STAND ALL THE WAY UP

Stories of Staying in It When You Want to Burn It All Down

Sophie Hudson

B&H
PUBLISHING
NASHVILLE, TENNESSEE

For David—
You lived this book with me,
and I couldn't have written it without you.
I'm so glad we get to stand all the way up together.

Contents

All Manner of Monkey Business

⁂

Kenya, as it turned out, knew exactly what was up.

Kenya the country. Not Kenya Moore of *Real Housewives of Atlanta* fame, though I would be delighted to pay her a visit as well.

A couple of summers ago my son, Alex, and I went to Kenya (more about that later), and on the next to last day of our trip, we flew on a very tiny airplane to the Maasai Mara National Reserve.

For the record, there is nothing that encourages some deep reflection regarding your personal relationship with Jesus Christ like flying on a very tiny airplane. I daresay it might result in something resembling personal revival.

The plane, thankfully, landed safely, and we set out on a safari ride just minutes after we walked off the dirt runway. For a couple of hours we oooh'd and aaah'd over elephants and buffaloes and giraffes, and sometime around noon, we checked in at the place we were staying. It was actually an open-air lodge (here's a hot tip: whenever someone uses the phrase "open-air," that's code for "air-conditioning is unavailable"), and our rooms were understated but stunning tent structures. There was a wood floor and a bathroom in each tent, but the vaulted ceiling and back wall were canvas. This is why I am somewhat tempted to say that we were glamping, but that would mean that I have to use the word "glamping," so no.

After we hung out at the lodge for a few hours and "freshened up" (and by "freshened up" I mean plugging in my tent's hair dryer next to the bed and pressing the "cool" button for a half hour or so because FAN), we went on a second safari ride at dusk.

Here's what I have to say about that: Kenya, you are stunning.

You, too, Kenya Moore.

We headed back to the lodge after sunset (no joke: we actually had to wait for an elephant to get out of the middle of the road, and I am so sophisticated that all I could do in that moment was fight the urge to repeat "WEL-COME—to JURASSSSSSIC PARK" until someone threw me off our truck). Our group—nine of us, I think—went to dinner in the lodge's dining room, and I had just started to eat my potato and leek soup when one of the lodge's managers approached our table.

"I'm so sorry to interrupt," he said softly, in the most lovely, lilting Kenyan accent, "but which of you is staying in number 27?"

I continued eating my soup because I had no idea who was in number 27—until Alex tapped my knee and whispered, "Mama. We're in 27!"

"Oh!" I responded. "We're in 27!"

My friend Shaun immediately put his head in his hands and started to laugh—because he had the good sense to know that if the manager was at our table, this was bound to be the beginning of a *really* good story.

"Ma'am," the manager continued, "if I may ask you a question: do you have any medication that you might need in 27? Anything valuable?"

Rain was falling in sheets outside, and since we were in an open-air dining area, I was having a little trouble hearing what the manager was saying. I thought maybe I misunderstood.

"I'm sorry?" I said. "Medication? You want to know if I have any medication?" This struck me as an odd line of questioning.

"Well, ma'am," he replied very calmly, "it would seem, you see, that the, um, *monkeys* have gotten into your tent."

This part I heard loud and clear.

"What?" I asked, likely way too loudly. "THE MONKEYS?"

Shaun's head was now on the table. He was done.

"Yes, ma'am. The monkeys. And I wanted to make sure that you didn't have any medication in your bags—anything you might need before you go home."

I looked at Alex with my mouth hanging open, like somehow that was going to help me know what to say next. Finally I found my words.

"Well, I'm not worried about medication, but our passports? I'm very worried about our passports. We are going to need our passports."

We were flying home the next day, and all I could picture was a massive troop of monkeys, frolicking in the grassy area behind our tent, gleefully ripping our passports to shreds in the rain.

"Yes, ma'am," my good friend the manager replied. "Of course. Your passports. We have sent someone down to clean up the mess, but when you go back to your tent, please be sure to check your things and make sure your passports are there. Anything else, ma'am?"

He smiled as he said all of this. Because, you know, it was just an average Wednesday in the Maasai Mara.

"Just one thing," I replied, "if you don't mind me asking: how in the world did the monkeys get in our tent?"

"Oh!" he answered excitedly. "The monkeys are very clever!"

Sure. Of course they are. Those clever, industrious monkeys.

By the way, Shaun was almost passed out from laughter at this point. He had shifted to somewhere between the table and the floor while I, on the other hand, looked like I was the current national title-holder in the Blank Stare competition. I was not amused.

The manager went on to explain that the monkeys knew how to unzip the canvas windows, and apparently one of the windows in our tent had an unsecured zipper (which, as we all know, will always get you into trouble, but that's another topic for another time).

About twenty minutes later, when the rain had tapered off a bit and I had sufficiently pushed my food around my plate while I fretted about our passports, Alex and I walked down to our tent. Thankfully, everything looked normal. I had expected pillow feathers all over the floor and a monkey perched on the bathroom counter, eating our toothpaste, but apart from the fact that our bags were in slightly different places, everything looked almost like it had when we left for safari. I checked for our passports, and they were still tucked into the suitcase pocket where I left them, oh hallelujah.

I noticed that Alex's Dallas Cowboys cap had been moved to the other side of the room (I had no idea that Dak Prescott was so popular with Kenyan wildlife, but it stands to reason that his appeal is international), and when I picked it up, I saw one lone, semi-smashed pistachio shell underneath.

I got so tickled—and immediately understood that I had unknowingly and unintentionally lured the monkeys into our tent. I had packed a bag of pistachios just in case the food on safari wasn't great or we needed a snack, but I had no idea that our bag of Great Value pistachios would be such irresistible bait.

You live and learn, I guess.

It had been an eventful day in ways we had expected and ways we couldn't have imagined, so around 9:30, I double-checked the zippers on all the windows, and Alex and I went to bed.

The next morning we left the tent at sunrise—we were scheduled for a final, early morning safari ride—and as we were walking to the front of the lodge, one of the stewards stopped us.

"Was everything okay last night, ma'am?" he asked. "Did you sleep well?"

"Everything was great," I answered. "We slept *incredibly* well—and no more monkeys!"

We laughed, and he leaned in closer.

"Ma'am, I have to tell you. When we went into your tent yesterday evening? Ma'am, *clothes were strewn everywhere!*"

I thanked him for taking care of us, and Alex and I resumed our walk. We'd only traveled a few more steps down the stone path when I thought, *Well, if nothing else, that's a metaphor that will flat-out preach.*

It has continued to preach, as a matter of fact.

Because my goodness. For the last three or four years—the second half of my forties—the proverbial monkeys have been all up in my business. Throwing things around. Disrupting my life. Messing up my stuff. Eating my pistachio nuts (okay, maybe not so much that, but for the record I don't love it if people help themselves to my snacks). I haven't written much about it because I've been doing super important things like watching *The Great British Baking Show* on Netflix and compiling an exhaustive cross-city reference guide for the *Real Housewives* series (not really, but I totally could) and getting trapped in an endless social media labyrinth composed primarily of random

Instagram stories mixed with novel-length Twitter threads. Diversion is time consuming, y'all.

Then there's this: on top of all the real-live life that has come in hot, as the kids would say, there's the cold, hard fact that this stage of life can be sort of weird. Maybe that's because many of us are still twenty-seven in our heads, so we face the ongoing challenge of reconciling who we think we are (young! fresh faced! know the words to every song on the radio!) with who we actually are (middle aged! wrinkled! dependent on '80s and '90s music for any sort of singalong!). Plus, after you hit the post-thirties part of your life, you're usually past the excitement of most of the big firsts: first big move, first real job, first house, first nephew, first child, first church you choose, first lots of other delightful moments.

And while sure, there's something to be said for having some experience and wisdom under your belt, there are also endless opportunities for humility and disappointment. Maybe your marriage doesn't work out like you hoped, or your stomach has forgotten how to be flat, or you feel disillusioned by what used to fill you with hope, or your attempts to balance a full-time job with caring for elderly parents leave you frustrated, or you try to do the latest viral dance craze at your kids' Homecoming pep rally and nobody in your family will speak to you anymore.

Which reminds me.

One night last year I was driving home from church with Alex, who was a high school freshman at the time, and I said, "Hey, do you know what song I like right now?"

"What song?" he answered.

"Oh, gosh," I replied. "I can't think of the guy who sings it. He's young? And his picture on his album is like two halves of a face? Oh, what is his name . . . I cannot remember . . . but I think the song is called 'Tokyo,' maybe?"

Alex pulled out his phone so that he could survey his entire digital music library in 4.7 seconds. Then he laughed and shook his head.

"Mama. MAMA. It's Shawn Mendes, and the song is 'Lost in Japan.'"

"That's right. 'Tokyo.' Just like I said."

"MAMA."

And scene.

This is exactly what I'm talking about, y'all.

Nobody told me that middle age would leave me quite so challenged in the area of pop culture.

I OBJECT, YOUR HONOR.

If you think about it, the middle of anything is sort of notoriously taxing, isn't it? I mean, nobody's really writing poems about the awesomeness of middle school, and the middle of, say, labor and delivery is when most women could get on board with some more comfortable/enjoyable options for bringing that little bundle of joy into the world. The starting and finishing, those are easier; the former is energizing, and the latter is rewarding. But the really long stretch in the middle—the part where we're all asking if we're there yet—it can seem sort of endless and thankless and maybe even a little bit pointless. That's where endurance gets tough.

But.

As difficult as these last few years have been—as deeply as they have challenged me—I'm more aware than ever that these are the days. This is the time the Lord has ordained for me to live and love and give Him glory. Sure, these days have marked a humbling, refining stretch of life. But these days have also been wonderful in ways I never could have imagined.

And somewhere in the middle of all this middle, the Lord has been showing me <u>what it looks like to *stand*.</u> To stand in my own life, to stand for the unheard or unseen, to stand for the generation behind me, to stand for the cause of Christ, and to stand all the way up even when what I really want to do is get back in the bed and pretend like everything is just fine and there's nothing I can do to help.

You would have never convinced me of this even five years ago, but the standing is turning out to be my favorite. And for the first time, I think, I want to write about what I've been learning. I want to laugh about it, too. I'm not trying to change anybody's mind or convince anyone to see things the way I do. Because sure, I'm standing, but I'm not on top of a soapbox; I'm just sharing some stories because, as it turns out, the monkeys have taught me some things.

My hope is that you'll relate to the funny and the serious and the ridiculous and the heartbreaking and everything in between. And maybe, just maybe, you'll find yourself a little more motivated to stand up and make it through whatever your particular middle happens to be.

One more thing before I forget.

Those pistachios in our tent? The ones the actual monkeys found so appealing?

They were Cajun-flavored, my friends.

Oh, yes, they were. Not exactly the flavor profile of the average Masaai Mara monkey.

If I had to guess, I would say that as much as those monkeys may have been living it up in our tent, they were likely ready to burn it all down (digestively speaking, of course) after those Cajun-flavored pistachios settled in. It was likely a long night for our beloved Kenyan simians.

Rest assured that this book won't be quite that spicy.

I sure am glad that you're here.

CHAPTER 1

Welcome at the Gate

So I don't know what sort of fancy festivities you enjoyed this past New Year's Eve—what sparkly frock you selected for toasting and dancing and revelry-ing—but as for me and my house, we were in our soft pants at home. This is no different from every other New Year's Eve of my married life, because we always stay home and we always wear soft pants. I blame this practice (staying home, not wearing the soft pants) on my daddy, who spent most of my teenage years reminding me that the roads are a dangerous place on July 4th and New Year's Eve, thereby conditioning me to be home on major holidays by 2:30 p.m. at the latest.

This year, David and I did invite some people to join us, though— our friends Stephanie and Joey came over for supper and Spades—but by 11 o'clock everybody was stretching and yawning and content to leave the midnight merriment to Anderson Cooper and the folks in Times Square. Alex was away at a youth retreat, so we didn't even have to go through the motions with some Roman candles and sparklers. By 11:30 the Coonses had gone home, David was asleep, and I was scrolling through our DVR in the hopes of saying good-bye to 2018 with the help of at least one of my favorite Egg Bowl games from years past.

Judge away, y'all. I promise it won't bother me. I walk in SEC football freedom.

I finally climbed in the bed around 12:45, but sleep wouldn't come. I kept thinking about different moments from our night (I am happy to tell you that I had cooked the collard greens of my life), and eventually that gave way to a 2018 highlights reel playing in my brain. I was just about to doze off—right on the verge of sleep—when my eyes flew open and I awkwardly propped myself up on one elbow.

This is it, I thought. *This is the year I turn fifty.*

Then I was wide awake.

Because, you see, fifty has been hovering in the back of my mind for the longest time—and now, well, it was officially upon us.

So I laid there, and I wondered how I could possibly be so close to fifty, and I thought about how fast it all goes. I thought about how vividly I remember being fourteen and twenty-one and thirty-five and forty-two. I thought about how in so many ways I'm the same person I've always been. I thought about how I cried when I turned nineteen because it was the last year of being a teenager, and now I'm wide awake on New Year's Eve because I'm forty-nine and don't want to say good-bye to the last decade of my life.

Apparently, I have issues with birthdays where a "9" rolls over to "0."

There's some history to my stand-offish relationship with fifty. My mama gave birth to me, her third and final child, when she was in her late thirties, and while I realize the late thirties are now when lots of women start to think about maybe wanting to have their first child, the 1960s were a different day. Mama was in her forties when I started kindergarten, and by the time I was in second grade, when it seemed like lots of other mamas were barely pushing thirty, Mama was wearing reading glasses in the after-school pick-up line. I noticed. In retrospect, big deal—and ROCK ON WITH YOUR BURNT SIENNA READERS, OUIDA SIMS—but at the time I thought it would be awesome if Mama was just a little younger. I wanted her to wear a bathing suit at the pool instead of her sensible shorts (Mama only had one pair of shorts because she did not enjoy being bare-legged) and her cotton shirt. Looking back, I can appreciate that Mama was actually the picture of contentment and self-acceptance—she knew who she was and what she was working with and did not need anyone else's approval, *thank you very much*—but when I was in junior high and Mama turned fifty, I internalized the (inaccurate) perception that fifty was, like, SUPER old.

So I assumed that when I turned fifty—way off in the far distant Jetsons-ish future, when I would no doubt be living in some sort of space pod—I would also be, like, SUPER old. Keep in mind that when I was a teenager, I would hear people mention that they were in their fifties and then feel straight-up sorry for them. I mean, I didn't walk up to them and say, *It must make you sad, all the age*, but I would feel silently thankful for my youth and my vim and my vigor, not to mention my wrinkle-free face. I couldn't imagine a day when I would look in the mirror and see parentheses around my mouth, though now I can say with confidence that the day is here, and by the way, the parentheses do not play.

If you're feeling adventurous you could even rappel from top to bottom of those things (at your own peril, of course).

However, the good news is that each parenthesis is about seven feet deep, so there's plenty of room to set up camp in there if you need to rest.

The upside, I guess, is that my feelings about fifty have changed. I look up to my fifty-plus friends like crazy. I love their wisdom, their confidence, their style—the whole thing. I want to move through the rest of my life with that level of ease. But where I get hung up—what catches in my chest a little bit—is the ever-increasing realization that time is getting away from me. There's just not near enough of it left, and fifty forces me to confront that.

So. I have a lot of feelings connected to fifty.

And I may not have I mentioned it, but I turn fifty this year.

Fifty. Years. Old.

Half a century.

Are you picking up on the fact that it's a little hard for me to believe?

A couple of years ago, when I was just a wee babe of forty-seven, Alex and I went to Kenya.

I mentioned that in the introduction. Monkeys, pistachios, etc.

Well, a couple of days before we went on safari and the monkeys ransacked our belongings, we were still in Nairobi, and we had plans to visit a community that was perched on the side of a cliff overlooking the Rift Valley. I was somewhat skeptical about the trip because of the events of the previous day. We had visited a Maasai tribe that lived over an hour from the nearest paved road, and I made the grave mistake of sitting in the very back row of the safari vehicle, which led to a bout of car sickness that left me skittish about any future off-road excursions.

It was an unenjoyable ride on several levels.

First, there was a great deal of bouncing in that safari vehicle— more bouncing than a woman of a certain age could be expected to handle with any degree of dignity. On top of that, the terrain was rough—like are-they-secretly-filming-us-for-a-truck-commercial rough—and I wasn't mentally prepared for it. There was also a great deal of swerving at varying rates of speed. At first I tried to be cheerful, thinking that our four-wheel Tilt-a-Whirl excursion couldn't last for much longer. But by the forty-minute mark of our trek, I had abandoned all pretense of pleasantries and had become nonverbal, which, you know, is a rare occurrence for me. By the sixty-minute mark, I was holding on to the seat in front of me for what felt like dear life, trying to find a fixed point outside the front window to steady my motion sickness concerns, and by the eighty-minute mark, I was wiping tears off my cheeks and telling the Lord that I would serve Him forever in the Rift Valley because there was no way I would be repeating that dirt road ride ever again.

Needless to say, after we returned to Nairobi that night, I was reluctant to get in another safari vehicle the next day and travel to another remote area. Because here's the deal: of all the things I had hoped to do in Kenya, vomiting in a car wasn't super high on the list. A good night's sleep turned out to be a decent enough reset from the Maasai travel madness, however. So on the Monday morning we were scheduled to visit to the community on the side of the cliff (oh, you could say "at the top of a mountain," but my danger radar was dialed all the way up to MAY DIE SOON, so "cliff" works great, thanks), I decided to be a trooper and tough it out, no matter how bad the drive might be.

My mama didn't raise no fool, though. I sat in the front row passenger's seat for day two of Kenyan off-roading. My equilibrium and I needed an unimpeded view of what was ahead.

Mercifully, the ride—though as rough as the previous day's—was only about twenty minutes long. The terrain started to even out as we got close to the top of the mountain, and as we all craned our necks to take in the houses and gardens and small businesses around us, our driver parked next to a brick wall that ran alongside the church we were visiting. I learned from my previous trips with Compassion that you never really know what a day is going to hold, so it's better to let go of expectations and just roll with whatever comes.

That being said, what happened next was the most wonderful surprise.

We could hear that something was going on before we could actually see it. People were singing—where, exactly, we couldn't tell—but as we moved closer to the church gates, the voices grew louder. Finally, as we turned the corner, we saw about forty women dancing in a loose formation, moving in our direction, singing worship songs at the top of their lungs. It was a stunning sight. Each woman was wearing a colorful cape tied around her neck, but more noticeable than the capes were the smiles. These women were beaming as they welcomed us, and as they moved closer, I could tell that most of them were carrying babies on their backs. Some were also carrying toddlers in their arms.

The women grabbed our elbows and pulled us into their group, patiently showing us how to move our feet and arms as we sang our way to the sanctuary. I imagine that from the sky we would have looked like a giant, brightly-clad amoeba inching its way across the dirt courtyard, the edges expanding and caving and expanding again depending on the direction of our movement. We were almost to the sanctuary door when I thought, *Wait! Where's Alex?*—and I wondered if he was hanging back, too shy to get in the mix of praise dancing with a group of Kenyan mamas he had never met before. I finally spotted him several yards behind me, his hands draped over the shoulders of the woman in front of him, his feet moving with the music—and as he turned his head, I could see that he was grinning ear-to-ear with the delight of it all.

It was a moment, y'all.

We eventually made our way into the sanctuary, giddy from the welcome and the joy of being united in worship. The church provided a variety of beverages for us, so everyone grabbed a soda or water or hot tea before we sat down for introductions and a word from the pastor. A lady named Mary was in charge of Compassion's ministry to mothers in that particular community, and when she stood up to explain what our day would hold, she greeted us on behalf of the church, recounted how the women had led us in worship from the second we stepped on church grounds, and she said something that resonated in my heart as much as it did in my ears:

"In Kenya, we hope you know that you are welcome at the gate."

You are welcome at the gate.

My brain instantly bookmarked her words.

You are welcome at the gate.

It's been two and half years since Alex and I visited that church. Two and a half years, and Mary's words still echo in my soul.

———————

So my forties and I, we're in the home stretch.

On a lot of levels, I'm sad to tell my forties goodbye. It probably sounds strange, but I feel like we're a couple of BFFs who can't bear to leave one another at the end of summer camp. We really hit it off when I was around forty-two and stopped operating out of fear so much of the time, and since then my forties and I have taken a lot of chances, laughed an obnoxious amount, cried as often as necessary, and high-fived more than might be considered normal. We have decided once and for all that there are few things we enjoy more than some simple pleasures: a family road trip, an ice-cold pitcher of Crystal Light lemonade, a really good college football game, a folding chair under a tailgate tent, a fall night on a back porch, a summer afternoon at the lake, a lunch with friends that stretches to the two-hour mark, and a high school lacrosse match on an early April evening.

This is the stuff, my friends.

This last decade hasn't been perfect or even idyllic—not by a long shot. For sure there have been mistakes and also regrets. From time to time I've gotten too big for my britches (literally and figuratively, AMIRITE), and the last few years have also been challenging in ways I didn't necessarily expect. There have been injuries, illness, loss, and my dear friend delayed grief—to the point that when grieving finally kicked in, I wondered if I needed to wear one of those MedicAlert necklaces so people would know what was going on with me.

She's grieving! And she can't get up!

It's interesting. I think one reason I've loved my forties is because even though it hasn't been easy, I've been less resistant to learning the lessons than I was when I was younger. And hands down one of the biggest lessons has been that sometimes, when the Lord puts me in a place of change or transition—when He's moving me from one thing to the next—I can be quick to panic, to manipulate, to control, to resist, to fight, to complain, and to question.

It's a side of myself I've seen far too often in these last few years—a time when the Lord has let me sit in some heartache and disappointment, a time when He has been teaching me to see things as they actually are and not as I wish they might be.

So here's what that has looked like: I've mourned the deaths of people I love and have tried to wrap my heart around living in a world without them. I've sometimes parented out of fear instead of conviction—over-analyzing and worrying as if that might actually make a difference—and in moments of great impatience, I've tried to boss my own child into repentance even though we all know that *never* works. I've minimized the work it takes to keep a marriage healthy and loving. I've been quick to dismiss ideas that aren't mine and to criticize philosophies I don't share. I've been angry with the evangelical church (that I love) and frustrated with my country (that I love). I've seen hatred hiding in places I thought were sacred, which means I've had to consider the ways I've been complicit in ignorance and injustice and oppression. I've wrestled with my pride, I've been humbled by how often I've failed, and I've contemplated the bottomlessness of my selfishness. I've talked so much more than necessary, knowing that there are still so many places where I need to listen and learn.

And for better or worse, in some ways that embarrass me and some ways that make me proud, my forties and I have confronted all of those things standing eyeball-to-eyeball. We've tried our best to work it on out.

We've worked it on out despite broken bones and hormone surges and a bladder that can no longer be trusted. We've settled down and settled in and committed to real-live life in ways I couldn't have fathomed ten years ago. We've (mostly) said good-bye to the angst-y comparison of my thirties and the approval seeking of my twenties. My forties have centered on asking some big questions and figuring out how to make my peace with the answers.

So yes. The last several years have been filled with transition. Change. Uncertainty. Gates galore, you might say.

But my Kenyan friend Mary was right.

Time after time, I was welcome at the gate.

And time after time, Jesus met me there.

So. Fifty.

Fifty? I'm not sure how to explain it. Fifty feels like something else. There's a part of me that feels like fifty is Sally O'Malley and a red polyester pantsuit and a series of awkward movements while I declare that I like to KICK and STRETCH and KICK. Fifty is Aurora Greenway wearing a dress with a maybe-too-low neckline while she rides in a convertible with her astronaut neighbor and tries to remember how to be flirtatious.

But a bigger part of me knows that looking to fictional characters isn't the best way forward. I try to remind myself that my best friends from college also turn fifty this year, so I'm in great company. But still, fifty can't possibly be me, right? Surely I would have received more warning. Granted, my left knee does get sort of stuck in one spot thanks to that time I slipped on the wet floor of the junior high gym when I was chaperoning the high school Christmas Dance—so I'm often reminded that my joints are not fresh and springy and new—but as long as I've iced my knee enough and steer clear of deep knee bends, I would swear under oath that I'm not a day over thirty.

I AM STILL SUCH A YOUNG THING.

Maybe?

No?

Whatever.

Nonetheless, there's no turning back. And as my friend Melanie mentioned to me a couple of weeks ago, turning fifty sure beats the alternative.

So as I walk (okay, I'm limping a tiny bit, but THAT KNEE, y'all) toward fifty, here's what I'm trying to remember: when we're moving through a figurative gate in our lives—whether that's a change in perspective, a change in family dynamics, a change in career, a change in age, or whatever—the Lord is working. He's teaching. He's not just changing our circumstances; He's changing *us*. After all, when we look at gates in Scripture, it's clear that they were places where *things were happening*—whether that was Boaz's redemption of Ruth (Ruth 3), Mordecai's discovery of an assassination plot (Esther 2), Abraham's purchase of Sarah's tomb (Genesis 23), or Jesus' statement in John 10 that He is the gate. Things got *settled* at gates in Scripture: community matters, personal matters, even judicial matters were addressed, argued, and decided at the gate.

The same is true right here, right now—just in a more metaphorical sense. So maybe—just maybe—as I'm facing this big 5-0 transition and battling the temptation to mimic some quality '80s song lyrics and ask "What have I / What have I / What have I done to deserve this?"— I'm missing a much bigger, much more important idea.

God has invited me to another gate.

And I am welcome.

And He will settle some things when I get there.

I'm not sure what the Lord has in store for this next decade. Well, I do know that I'll have to start having colonoscopies and that feels unfair since I have only recently gotten used to the annual squeezing and flattening known as the mammogram.

I feel confident about this, however: there will be plenty of places down the road where the Lord will refine me, teach me, and challenge me. Just like the last ten years, there will be gates aplenty. So—if the Lord would have it—I'm going to carry my Kenyan friend Mary's words into fifty, into sixty, and beyond. *I am welcome at the gate.* No matter the transition or hardship or change that's ahead of me, I'm welcome there. And no doubt I will remember the beautiful June day we spent at a church perched on a cliff overlooking the Rift Valley, and I'll sing and dance and worship my way into whatever is ahead.

As long as this knee doesn't seize up on me.

I like to KICK, after all.

We are welcome at the gate

CHAPTER 2

Life Is Frequently Very Glamorous

I hate being late.

Oh, I know. I just used the "h" word. But it is so appropriate in this instance.

Because I really do despise being late. I loathe being late. I want to punch being late in the face.

I've been this way as long as I can remember, but it really kicked into high gear when I was fifteen and started to drive. I was happy to be the nerd sitting outside your house at 6:45 for our 7 o'clock study session, because I'll tell you what was not an option for me: walking in at 7:02. That kind of reckless behavior was simply unacceptable, and I would have no part in it.

I'll tell you something else, too: I have no problem taking my seat in the sanctuary at 2:15 if your wedding starts at 3:00. You might think that is too much idle time, but here's what I will tell you: I will be settled, and I will be at peace, and I will not be scrambling for a seat at 2:55. I will be happy to read your wedding program for a half hour, scrutinize the names of your bridesmaids and groomsmen to see if I know any of their parents *(oh, the maid of honor's name is Mary Watson McMullen, and I went to college with a Sally Watson, so PERHAPS THEY ARE RELATED)*, and analyze the facial expressions of all relatives as they are seated to see if everybody's as happy about this union as they say they are.

But inasmuch as I can control it, I will not be tardy.

Somewhere in the recesses of my memory is a conversation I once had with my father, and in that conversation Daddy said, "Being late is like telling folks that your time is more valuable than theirs." Daddy no doubt shared hundreds of nuggets of wisdom with me when I was in high school and college—things like, "It's not okay for your friends to leave an actual stop sign in your bedroom because removing a stop sign from an intersection is a crime" (this actually happened), and "Paying a bank overdraft fee is the dumbest use of your money there is" (ditto). I didn't pay a whole lot of attention to those admonitions (Daddy returned the "misplaced" stop sign to the police station), (I was a slow financial learner), but if the topic was timeliness, I was as compliant and obedient as could be. Being early eliminates the risk that someone will be frustrated or annoyed by my late arrival, not to mention that I save myself from feeling rushed or stressed or embarrassed. You might disagree, of course, but I think being early is the business.

This is never more true than when I travel.

The irony is that I am married to someone who would be perfectly content to stroll up to the gate at 12:58 p.m. for a 1:00 p.m. flight. I, on the other hand, am going to arrange my day so that I sit down at my gate at least at least sixty minutes before the time we're supposed to board. I don't care if the airport is only twenty-five minutes from my house; I'm going to leave (typically) 2½ hours before my flight because what if there's a wreck on the way to the airport? What if there are no parking spaces in the garage? What if the line to check a bag is longer than expected? What if a flight is unexpectedly canceled? What if TSA only has one person moving people through security? How did I even marry someone who isn't even *a tiny bit* motivated by these harrowing scenarios?

CAN THIS MARRIAGE BE SAVED?

Fortunately, David and I have been able to work out most of our travel differences, and that is because he has given up any hope that I will become a reasonable human being where travel time is concerned. I have worn him down. In fact, this past summer, when we were going to New York City and leaving on a 6:00 a.m. flight, the night before our trip he said, "Hey. What time do you want to leave in the morning? Midnight?"

"That sounds fine," I replied. Neither of us batted an eye.

Then we laughed. And I'll have you know that we actually left the house at 3:45. Look how breezy and reasonable I am!

More often than not, though, when I'm traveling, I'm alone. Five or six times a year I fly to another state for a speaking engagement or some sort of book/podcast eventery, and on those trips I get to practice my beloved earliness with great enthusiasm. For me this is soul medicine. Last November there was even a day when my friend Melanie, who was about to drive home to San Antonio, dropped me off at the airport in Houston despite the fact that my flight didn't leave for about six hours. I was so early to the airport that I couldn't check my bag or go through security yet—I had a couple of hours to kill—so I said goodbye to Mel, walked to the far end of the ticketing area, and set up shop in a corner of a barbecue restaurant. I answered email, I invoiced podcast ads, I ate an early lunch, I watched college football, I texted with a couple of friends, and I started reading a new book.

Basically, I enjoyed a full vacation before I ever made it to my gate. Behold, efficiency!

Less than a week after my Saturday at the Houston Hobby International Resort, I flew out of Birmingham again and headed back to Texas. This time I was going to speak at a church in Dallas, so I left for the airport about 2½ hours before my flight, just as the good Lord intended. I parked in my favorite part of the garage (it's 5C if you're taking notes for future Birmingham travel), grabbed my suitcase, hopped on the elevator, and checked my bag at the Southwest counter. Sure, it was just a one-night trip, and my bag was pretty small, but you'd better believe that I checked it.

Why, you might wonder? This is because I despise—YES, I SAID "DESPISE"—carrying my luggage onto a plane. I mean, aren't we all enduring enough indignities by being herded at the gate like cattle and then crammed into a metal tube where we sit on top of one another while sipping 1.4 ounces of our favorite Coca-Cola product and twisting the air vent knob in an attempt to create a suggestion of a breeze? I'm not really sure why, on top of all that, we choose to participate in a system that requires us to hoist our luggage above our heads and wedge it into a bread box, but I'm going to offer a hearty "no, thanks" to that whole process. It's uncivilized, it slows boarding to a crawl, and it enables folks who confuse the terms "carry-on" and "steamer trunk" to continue to make bad choices.

As I've already mentioned, I'm almost fifty years old. I am all the way done with enabling.

Basically, what I'm saying is that checking your bags is loving your neighbor, and if we want to be more like Jesus, let's just go ahead and accept that as the Lifter of our burdens, Jesus would have no part of a carry-on luggage situation.

Why are you shouldering that 48-pound duffel, friend? Lay it down at the ticket counter. Drop the rock! Walk in freedom!

When I finally got on my flight to Dallas, I was fighting some serious mixed emotions about going out of town. I've worked at the same school in Birmingham for the last nineteen years—fourteen as an English teacher, the last five as Dean of Women—and my school's football team was playing in the 5A State Championship that night. I was sick about missing it. Now granted, I had no idea we'd make it all the way to State when I agreed to speak in Dallas, but that was small comfort on a day when I left my school people and all their spirited revelry so that I could languish with the B boarding group and beg the Lord to spare me the sanctifying fire of a middle seat. I ended up finding a window seat at the back of the plane, and as I settled in for my trip to Houston and then to Dallas (I do not pretend to understand airlines and their connecting flight formulas), I popped in my earbuds, turned on the Leslie Odom Jr. Christmas album, and promptly fell asleep. Better to doze than to feel all my State Championship FOMO feelings.

The flight from Houston to Dallas was uneventful, apart from the Very Loud Talkers seated behind me and the fact that I'm pretty sure a man across the aisle from me took off his shoes during our flight. Granted, maybe I'm old-fashioned about this sort of thing, but I tend to think that removing your shoes during a flight is a fine way to communicate BY THE WAY, I LOATHE YOU ALL to your fellow travelers. I feel the same way about folks who tuck a foot-long Spicy Italian sandwich in the seatback pocket while they're listening to the safety instructions, then set about the business of unwrapping that coldcut treasure during take-off. I understand that travel days are long and a package of honey roasted peanuts might not get the job done in terms of providing daily sustenance, but what I am going to tell you is that a Spicy Italian is going to make its presence known a couple of different times on Flight 4036: first of all when Kevin in 11D unwraps it and inhales it in four bites, and second of all when Kevin experiences some post-Spicy Italian gastrointestinal discomfort about the time that we hit a cruising altitude of 35,000 feet.

It's one thing to eat a sandwich on a flight. It's a whole other deal to trap your fellow passengers in the unrelenting fog of your silent toots, Kevin.

Do better, Kevin.

After we landed in Dallas, I made a beeline for baggage claim, picked up my bag, then hopped on the rental car shuttle. I was speaking in a Dallas suburb about fifteen miles from the airport, and my plan was to check in my hotel, find somewhere to eat lunch, and maybe even get a manicure before I left for the church around five. I'm always slightly intimidated when I drive on Texas interstates—particularly in the bigger cities—because they look less like roads and more like someone aimed giant cans of Silly String at the ground and said, *This. This will be our roadway system.* The combination of frontage roads and access roads and exit ramps creates a concrete maze that I struggle to navigate even with the aid of Google Maps and Waze and other assorted apps that practically scream, "HERE! TURN RIGHT HERE, DUMMY! WHAT IS SO DIFFICULT ABOUT A RIGHT TURN? A 90-DEGREE ANGLE IS STILL A 90-DEGREE ANGLE IN TEXAS! GET IT TOGETHER!"

Mercifully, though, I made it to my exit and my hotel with little difficulty, and after I checked in, I drove to the closest shopping center because, well, there was a Chipotle there, and it is the finest of all the fast-casual restaurants. Sure, I take issue with their queso (and we all should, for it is somehow powdery and runny at the same time), but their rice options/meats/vegetables/salsas/toppings/chips are fantastic. Plus, I was still feeling bummed about missing the state championship game—not to mention that the day's news headlines had wrapped me in a bit of a funk—so a Chipotle bowl seemed like a comforting lunchtime treat. Even when you're missing your people and wondering when politics in our country became such a violent sport, Chipotle's guacamole does not disappoint.

After lunch I still had a few hours before I needed to be at the church, so I hopped in my sassy rental sedan and drove across the parking lot to a nail salon. My fingernail polish was in a bit of a 911 situation, so it seemed like a good use of time to let a professional step in and administer the necessary care. What I didn't stop to think about was the deep level of awkward and borderline loneliness I might feel as the sole customer in an unfamiliar nail salon in an unfamiliar strip mall in an unfamiliar town. A language barrier prevented much small talk or casual conversation, and while I'm not saying that the silence was deafening, exactly, it was noticeable enough that the nail technician stopped my manicure so she could turn on the TV and let an afternoon talk show keep me company.

Every once in a while, my phone would light up with a text from Alex about the upcoming football game back at home. It was bitterly cold in Alabama, and he was trying to round up everything he needed before he rode over to Tuscaloosa with our friends, the Thompsons. When I had a free hand, I would type a quick message to remind him *yes, do* take a pair of gloves with you, and *no,* for the love, *do not* take a cowbell into the game (this is an ongoing refrain in our Mississippi State home, this harsh reality that cowbells are not welcome in all athletic venues), but mostly I just contemplated the view outside the nail salon windows: a tower of stacked interstate to my left, a parking lot straight ahead, and the profile of a Costco to my right.

The familiar vista of longleaf pine trees, Bermuda grass, and crepe myrtle-lined roadways was hundreds of miles away, and I felt every last one of them.

Fortunately, though, I wasn't in Texas to find comfort in the scenery. I was there to spend some time with the women at a local church, and after I left my manicure, I couldn't wait to get back to the hotel, change clothes, and meet the folks I had traveled to see. Finding connection and camaraderie in local churches—regardless of where that church is located—has been an unexpected encouragement over the last few years, and no matter the size of the church, no matter the reason the women are gathering, no matter what I'm there to do, I get obnoxiously jazz hands-y about getting to serve them in some small way. So even though I was bummed about missing the football game, and even though I was registering higher than normal on the homesick scale, I couldn't wait to finally get where I was going.

When I arrived at the church, I pulled into the parking lot and sat in the car for a few minutes to pray before I went inside. I noticed when I turned off the car that there was a warning message on the dashboard—"Key Battery Low"—but I didn't think too much of it. I restarted the car to make sure the key fob was still working, and with the fresh assurance that all was well, I turned off the car for the second time, grabbed my purse, Bible, and iPad, and walked to the church entrance.

Within four seconds of walking in the door, the ladies greeted, welcomed, and hugged me before they offered a quick tour to help me get my bearings. We also did sound check, where I discovered that the headset microphone probably wasn't going to work for me because, well, my head is enormous—the circumference of a medium-sized watermelon. Every time I turned my head to the right or to the left I feared that the back of the headset was going to break apart, and this, my friends, is why I will forever and always prefer a handheld microphone. Not only is it impartial to those of us with oversized noggins, it also doesn't make me feel like I need to channel early 2000's Britney

Spears midway through a talk and break down some choreographed dance moves to "Oops, I Did It Again."

As I am wont to do.

So a handheld mic works for me on a couple of levels, I guess.

After sound check my hosts took me to a room where I could look over my notes, and after I did that a few times, the rest of the evening passed in a blur. I visited with a friend from high school, then moved to the sanctuary for worship and the night's program. I tried to be supersubtle about checking my phone for the football score, but when it was time for me to talk, I fessed up that I asked Alex to send me score updates and might occasionally be looking at my watch as texts came in. Luckily Texas understands my brand of football crazy, particularly where state championships are concerned. #TexasForever.

As always, it was a blast to laugh with the women and be encouraged by Scripture together. It was close to nine by the time I climbed back in the rental car, and sadly, I had just gotten word that our team had lost the state title game. I was bummed for my people back home, but I still needed to grab something superfast for a late supper. I don't like to eat much before I speak, mainly because I feel like digestion can be noisy—and that's a legitimate distraction for others when you're holding a microphone. There weren't a whole lot of restaurant options near the church, so I pulled into a Taco Bell (only the finest cuisine will do), ordered Some Form of Nachos and a drink, then headed for the hotel. The key battery issue from earlier that night was nagging at the back of my brain—I would be leaving early the next morning for the airport and didn't have much of a window to tend to any car trouble—so I figured I had better call the rental company when I got to my room.

When I pulled into a parking spot at the Marriott Courtyard where I was staying, I was increasingly aware that my phone call to Alamo

was going to have to take a brief backseat to a trip to the restroom. I
didn't think I drank much while I was at the church, but based on the
level of, um, *urgency* I was experiencing, my bladder was at maximum
capacity. I threw the car into park, grabbed all of my stuff—which was
an armful after factoring in my recent Taco Bell purchases—and was
just about to open my door when I saw the warning: Key Battery Low.

Dang it.

It's fine, I told myself, *since I'm about to call the rental folks anyway,*
so I awkwardly tried to push open the door, stand up, and then close
the door without using my hands. However, the act of standing up
threw my bladder situation into sharp focus; I stood very still for a
few seconds, took several deep breaths, and reminded myself that it
wouldn't be *that* many steps to my hotel room. I started walking slowly
toward the front door of the hotel—like I was the maid of honor in a
bridal processional—and I was almost to the lobby doors when I realized that I hadn't locked the rental car. I pressed the button on the key
fob, which was still in my hand, but nothing happened.

Say it with me now: "Key Battery Low."

Deeply aggravated, I turned to take a few steps in the direction of
the car, thinking that maybe I was too far away, and after I walked
maybe ten feet, I realized that the situation with my insides had
moved from *Hey, you should probably go to the restroom soon* to ALERT,
ALERT, WE ARE IN A FOUR-ALARM SITUATION. I REPEAT:
WE ARE IN A FOUR-ALARM SITUATION.

I clicked the "lock" button on the key fob.

Nothing.

Which means I had a decision to make.

In what was maybe the most literal Sophie's Choice of my life-
time, I knew that I needed to either go to the restroom and then
check on the car—or go ahead and check on the car before I went to

the restroom. I was so tired, so ready to just be in my room for good already, so I decided I might as well deal with the car since I was already in the parking lot. Thankfully there wasn't anyone around to witness my awkward attempts at Car Maintenance While Practicing Bladder Control, so I very carefully inched closer to my parking space, baby step after baby step, not wanting to drop what I was carrying and also *not wanting to drop what I was carrying, if you catch my drift.* When I was finally standing in front of the car, I clicked the key fob again.

Nothing.

As delicately and gingerly as I could, I stepped down from the sidewalk to the pavement. I wanted to see if I could get the key fob to open the trunk, so I tippy-toed (carefully!) to the back of the car. All the while, the lower half of my body was screaming at me. The key fob didn't work on the trunk, either, so I put everything I was holding in my arms—purse, Bible, iPad, Taco Bell bag, drink—on top of the trunk, and, with my arms finally freed, I braced myself against the side of the car for a round of deep breathing exercises. I knew that my next step was to see if I could get the car to crank—if the key fob would communicate with the start button—and I didn't want my bladder to betray me when I sat down in the driver's seat and thereby altered my level of elevation.

In a way, it was like a super intense Jenga game. Every single move carried the threat of utter collapse.

As I opened the driver's side door, I continued to breathe deeply and rhythmically, like Lamaze for the middle-aged woman who is just trying to hold on to some small shred of urinary dignity. I tried with all my might to keep the tops of my legs together as I flopped into the seat, and after I paused for another few seconds, knowing full well that I had pushed everything connected to my kidneys about as far as nature would allow, I put my foot on the brake and pushed the "start" button.

Nothing.

So this was really much worse than I had anticipated.

I sat there trying to figure out my next, best move, trying to make sense of how I was going to get to the airport early the next morning, wondering if I would ever sleep knowing that I had some car complications on my hands. Ultimately I decided that the next best step was to call the rental car company, which would have been so easy if my phone wasn't in my purse.

You know, on the trunk.

Given the amount of pressure making itself known in the lower half of my body, getting to my phone was going to require way more movement than I believed to be optimal. Nevertheless, I persisted. I eased myself out of the car with all the speed of a nonagenarian recovering from double hip replacement surgery, and I exhaled very dramatically before I shut the car door.

I was just about to turn in the direction of the trunk when my body began to notify me that it was no longer interested in my drawn-out negotiations.

Reader, a humbling was imminent.

I twisted from side to side like a glitched cartoon character, wondering where I should go considering what was happening, but it was increasingly clear to me that there was no "off" switch. There was no longer an option for me to run up to my room and handle the situation privately. I mean, I had known for the better part of fifteen minutes that between the malfunctioning key fob and the oppressive sense of urgency that something had to give, but what I didn't know was that the "something" would be my dignity.

Before I even fully realized what was happening, my body took charge of the situation. And that is why I stood right there in the Marriott Courtyard parking lot, right beside my rented Nissan Altima with the non-functioning key fob, and with the sobering knowledge that I had pushed my body further than it had ever intended to go, I laid down my pride on that pitch-black pavement and wet my pants like a champion.

I'll have you know that I wet my pants for what seemed like a full minute.

It wasn't a full minute, of course. I'm pretty sure that's scientifically impossible. But it was long enough that maybe the humiliation would have seemed to pass more quickly if someone had played some music or something. "Let It Go" would have been a good option.

For several seconds I stood stock still in the parking lot—just me, my unleashed bladder, and a pair of burgundy corduroys that deserved far better treatment than what they received on that chilly Thursday evening. When my preoccupation with the state of my bladder was over, however, I snapped to attention. I grabbed my stuff off the back of the trunk, I put my purse on my shoulder, and as quickly and stealthily as I could, I walked into the hotel lobby, somehow managing to evade even a glance from the gentleman working the front desk.

That was fine by me. What with my pants being soaked through like a toddler's romper and all.

I made it to my room, jumped in the shower, put a quick load of laundry in the sink (desperate times), and finally called the rental car company. The key fob fix was easy enough, but it did require me to return to the parking lot in my pajamas so I could make sure it worked. Given the walk of shame I enjoyed about fifteen minutes earlier, tending to car business in my nightclothes felt downright professional.

Behold the elegance, Marriott Courtyard patrons.

It was almost midnight when I finally turned out the light, and it was barely light outside when I woke up the next morning. I got ready in approximately seven minutes, rolled my bag to the car, and headed back down the interstate that I had traveled not even twenty-four hours before. There was no question that it had been an eventful trip. In the seventeen-plus hours I was in the Dallas area, I experienced all manner of FOMO, ate by myself in a strange Chipotle, wrestled with homesickness, sat through a weird manicure situation, lost a state championship game (well, I mean, I didn't actually play in the game, but you know what I mean), and tee-tee'd all over myself in a hotel parking lot.

So on the surface it might seem like a questionable use of time and energy.

The sun was still trying to work its way to full blast when I returned my rental car, and as I considered the (lack of) wisdom in not packing a coat, I huddled under the shuttle stop and waited for my ride to the terminal. My flight didn't leave for a couple of hours, but as always I was happy I didn't have to rush. I was grateful to put the unfortunate key fob situation behind me, and I was looking forward to a delicious grande flat white (three Equals, no shame about aspartame, extra hot) as soon as I made it through security.

Half an hour later, I was sipping that flat white at my gate when I received a text that school was canceled back in Birmingham. Many parts of the southeast had been hit by an unexpected wave of snow early that morning—even Houston, of all places—and since I had to fly to Houston before the final leg of my trip home, I wondered if the weather was going to affect my flights. Everything still seemed to be on schedule, though, and when I boarded my flight to Houston around nine, I was hopeful that all would be well.

When it comes to flying preferences, I am a window seat person, and as we were making our descent into Houston, I cracked open my window shade to get a look at the ground. A light coating of white covered the landscape in every direction—a surreal sight considering the typical Texas landscape—and as we touched down on the ground, I pulled out my phone and checked texts from a few friends who knew I was headed back to Birmingham and wanted to make sure I knew to drive slowly and safely after I got home. According to them, at least, our Magic City was quite the winter wonderland.

My second flight took off right on time, and when I finally saw Birmingham from the air, I got all up in my feels, as the kids would say. If Houston was coated in snow, then Birmingham had been blanketed, and to my eyes, she had never looked more beautiful. Since there was no ice on the ground, we landed with no issues at all, and after I picked up my bag from baggage claim (OH YOU KNOW I CHECKED THAT THING), I walked in the direction of the parking garage.

The air was brisk but damp—heavy, almost—and after I made it to my car in 5C, I stared at my beloved Birmingham skyline way off in the distance. The gray haze cloaked the sky, the clouds hung low, and our city's tallest buildings blended into the horizon almost like camouflage.

I couldn't get over how gorgeous it all was.

I drove home—slowly—with my radio turned down low. I had never seen Birmingham look quite so lovely, and around every curve, at the crest of every hill, after every turn, I no doubt sounded like an ice dancing commentator who was utterly carried away with the gracefulness of a performance:

"Absolutely exquisite."

"Well, that is stunning."

"THIS. IS. FANTASTIC."

And then: "Oh, Lord. We needed this."

For some reason that day makes me think of a Bible story I love, a story of a woman named Naomi who had a rough go of it for more than a few years (and who faced far worse circumstances than an uncooperative bladder in a hotel parking lot). Naomi moved to a foreign country, her husband died, her sons died, and she eventually returned to her homeland in a pretty broken state. All that loss had taken a toll. Her daughter-in-law Ruth was faithful to care for her, but life wasn't easy for them.

Naomi, to her credit, never gave up. She helped Ruth find a way to provide for them. She taught Ruth about Judean culture. She explained how Ruth could pursue redemption for her widowhood.

Naomi kept showing up. Kept standing up for her daughter-in-law. Kept hoping in the midst of heartache.

And at the end of the book of Ruth, the redemption of Naomi's family secured by Ruth's marriage to Boaz and the subsequent birth of their baby, Naomi held her grandson on her lap.

After all the disappointment and loss and pain, there was new life.

The baby's name was Obed. He was an unexpected, undeserved grace to Naomi's family at the end of a hard time.

And I guess that's what I want to tell you.

Sometimes life is weird. Sometimes, for reasons we don't fully understand, it's so much harder than we expect. Maybe you feel like you're missing out on something with the people you love most, or maybe you get caught in the crossfire of Kevin's Spicy Italian sandwich, or maybe life feels like one heartbreaking loss after another, or maybe your state gets turned inside out by a special Senate election and everybody hates each other, or maybe you get to talk to some nice people for a few hours and then wet your pants afterward.

Feel free to insert your own specific set of circumstances. Hopefully none of them involve soiling your clothes in a public setting.

But here's what I've learned—and here's where Naomi's story is such a good reminder. In the middle of all of those things—or in the middle of even worse things—something beautiful will surprise you. Something beautiful will be the grace of God when you're in a tough stretch.

And on a day when you expect it the least but just might need it the most, that beauty—well, it will move you a little further forward. And it will be enough.

So keep showing up. Keep standing up. For whatever it is—but especially in and for your own life. I would of course advise that you show up early—even a couple or six hours early—because you don't want to miss it.

You really don't.

Promise.

Keep showing up

CHAPTER 3

A Fine How-Do-You-Do

For as long as I can remember, I've been a big purse person. I like long straps, plenty of interior pockets, and enough room that I can slide in my laptop on a moment's notice.

Because as we all know, we often face situations where we need to find storage solutions for our electronics as quickly as possible.

Last year, however, I bought something smaller—namely, a wallet from one of my favorite local stores. And this wallet—well, I don't mean to overstate it—but it was everything I've ever wanted in my life. It had an outer pocket for the things I use most frequently—debit card, driver's license, Costco membership card, phone—and the wallet itself, when unzipped, would pretty much hold a week's worth of groceries. I kept my keys in there, all my store reward cards, stamps, cash, change, lipstick—you name it.

What? You're wondering if it also held an assortment of miniature succulents?

AS A MATTER OF FACT, IT DID.

The point is that I loved that orange wallet with my whole heart. It took great care of me, it wasn't expensive, it was deeply practical, and it broke me of my big purse habit.

By winter, though, the edges were starting to fray, and my orange friend, she was struggling. Coins were finding their way out of the wallet and onto the floor. This happened on approximately seventeen different trips to the grocery store when I reached for my debit card and inadvertently made it rain pennies, nickels, and dimes around my feet. Quarters couldn't escape quite yet, but it was only a matter of time.

For several weeks I walked through what can only be described as an existential crisis, desperately trying to figure out if I should buy another orange wallet or look for something else. Sure, there's something to be said for sticking with what you know—and I am one loyal somebody—but there are so many wonderful wallets out there, and I didn't want to be stiff-necked in the selection process.

In the end I concluded that I wanted to try something new in the handbags area of my life, so I began my search. You can even call it a quest if you want because my life is kind of boring and I don't get to participate in a whole lot of quests, so I think it's fair to consider my wallet search as quest-y.

As you can imagine, it was rife with adventure.

So for a couple of months (I'm embarrassed to admit that, but it's very accurate), whenever I was at a local store or department store or my beloved Nordstrom Rack (also known as The Mothership), I made a point to look through their wallet options, hoping to find a new friend. I had very specific criteria because I really needed the wallet to function as a small, handheld purse. I wanted a place for my keys to live, plenty of room for lipsticks and lip balm, plus all the stuff that enables me to make purchases and conduct my personal business.

In all honesty, I really don't know what sort of "personal business" I conduct. But saying that kind of makes me feel like a no-nonsense Congresswoman, someone who interrupts committee proceedings to say, "Gentlemen, we're going to have to dispense with this nonsense, this MOCKERY OF AMERICAN DEMOCRACY, because we are running behind schedule and we'd all like to be able to CONDUCT OUR PERSONAL BUSINESS before the end of the day."

Now I'm feeling pretty motivated, actually.

Anyway, I looked for a new wallet but didn't have much luck. I saw one I really liked when I was at a speaking event outside of Atlanta, and it's quite possible I overwhelmed the wallet's owner by asking a series of very enthusiastic questions like, "Where does your phone go?" "Oh! That is fantastic! Do you have room for lipstick? Keys?" "Where do you keep your cash? Can I see?"

That last question is where I likely went a step too far.

Late in the spring, though, I ran in Anthropologie to buy a candle, and I spotted some cute smaller bags propped up on a table. I picked up a few, unzipped them, and scrutinized every detail like I was shopping for a new car. Undecided, I walked away, and I was about to pay for my candle when I glanced over at the table again. The bright blue travel wallet was larger than I thought I wanted, but there was something about it I couldn't shake. So I abandoned my spot in line, set down my candle, and figured it wouldn't hurt to go for one more test drive.

And just in case you're thinking *Um, ma'am, I believe you're making more of this search than is necessary,* then let me just very gently say NO I AM NOT AND ALSO YOU ARE SO WRONG.

I'm a big proponent for healthy relationships, and make no mistake: a wallet is both a friend and a companion. It takes care of your stuff, and it's with you wherever you go. You have to be able to trust it—the relationship won't work if it indiscriminately drops your personal information at the feet of strangers—and you need to enjoy it because, well, you're going to spend a whole lot of time together. It will be with you at work, in restaurants, on vacation, in the car, and maybe most importantly in Nordstrom Rack.

(I realize that I am not the boss of you, but a trip to Nordstrom Rack is no time to mess around with subpar companionship.)

(If a friend is going to negatively affect the inherent joy of my Nordstrom Rack experience, then I'm going to have to seriously re-evaluate our relationship.)

(Good boundaries are important, everyone.)

The bright blue travel wallet looked like it might be able to meet my logistical and relational needs. The exterior was right up my aesthetic alley: bold color, an abstract map design on the front, and flecks of gold paint all over the place. Now that I'm describing it I realize it sounds like something that might live in Vegas, but somehow it was low-key and statement-making all at the same time. The interior was a yummy blush-colored suede, with a pocket for my phone, a pocket for a passport (which I wouldn't need, clearly, during the day-to-day, unless I unexpectedly needed to CONDUCT MY PERSONAL BUSINESS from a foreign land), and plenty of slots for my driver's license and assorted cards. I figured that I could tuck away my cash in the passport pocket, and there was definitely enough room for all of my lip care needs.

Once my decision was made, I was so excited to have found a new wallet BFF that I looked around to see if I knew even one other person in the store. I wanted more than anything to say, "I BELIEVE WE HAVE A WINNER," which is a sure sign that I was as overinvested in the wallet-buying process as I am when Mississippi State plays any sport at all.

Somebody is suiting up in maroon and white for a game of Tiddlywinks, you say?

I WILL BE RIGHT OVER.

So I bought the wallet for thirty-four American dollars, and y'all, over that first summer together we became so close. We went everywhere together and made some great memories, like finally trying Zumba at the gym, getting to know Pam, a lively LSU fan, during an hour-long wait in line at the SEC baseball tournament, and watching the new *Mission Impossible* movie in a theatre that has recliners.

It was a very special time. That stands to reason because it is, after all, a very special wallet.

A few months into our friendship, my wallet and I met my friend Mariel at Starbucks. Mariel graduated several years ago from the school where I work, and her grandparents have been like family to me since David and I moved to Birmingham nineteen years ago. I was so excited to catch up with her, but we immediately faced an unexpected challenge when we arrived at Starbucks: the unfortunate fact that lo, there was nary an open table inside.

This is not an optimal situation when it's July in Alabama. We decided to find a table outside, and in case you missed it, I will remind you that it was July in Alabama. I trust you will commend our bravery.

For the next twenty minutes or so, Mariel enjoyed her coffee, I enjoyed my iced flat white, and while my bright blue wallet wasn't enjoying a beverage, it certainly added to the beauty of our balmy surroundings. Mariel and I talked about her possible grad school options, we talked about her boyfriend's new job, and we were just starting to dig into some stuff about Jesus when a woman walked over to our table, looked at me, and said, "Ma'am? I am so sorry to bother you."

I'll be straight-up honest with y'all. My initial reaction was that she was going to tell me that she had read one of my books or listened to my podcast with Melanie. So I smiled, and I used my kind eyes, and I glanced over at Mariel to see if she seemed uncomfortable. I even tilted my head a little bit because that, everyone, is a sign that you are friendly and approachable.

I was preparing to ask the woman her name when she said, "I don't want to alarm you, but you have a really large cricket-type bug on your back."

So that immediately went in a different direction than I expected.

I twisted around, trying in vain to see what was on my back, and I said something along the lines of *Oh my gosh! Feel free to knock it off!* The woman initially declined my offer, saying she couldn't stand bugs so she didn't think she could touch it. Then she gestured for Mariel to stand up and look at the bug, too, while I shifted in my wrought iron chair and tried to read Mariel's expression for signs of imminent cricket-type bug danger. The two of them puzzled over the best strategy while I continued to sit there, in the heat, apparently hosting the tyrannosaurus of insects below my left shoulder, wondering how this whole encounter was going to play out.

After several seconds the woman spoke again. My hope was that she had come up with a bug removal plan after she chatted with Mariel, and to my relief, she had. Sort of. Because what she suggested to me was this: "Can I use your wallet to try to make the bug move?"

She was speaking of my bright blue wallet, of course. My dear friend.

And y'all, I can't explain why, maybe because I'm not really experienced in bug removal and couldn't think of a better solution, but in the interest of expediency and practicality, I very enthusiastically responded with "OF COURSE!"—like she had just offered me a fresh

scone or asked if I would like to sample one of Jo Malone's latest per-
fumes. And then I did what any rational person in my position would
have done: I turned back toward the table and lowered my shoulders so
it would be easier for the woman to, you know, smack me.

Rest assured that it was a whole new level of personal business
between my wallet and me.

So the woman picked up Bright Blue, and before I could think to
say, "MA'AM, THIS IS A TERRIBLE IDEA," she began to wallop me
across the back, all the while telling me how sorry she was to be hitting
me repeatedly right there on the Starbucks patio. It was an incredibly
surreal experience, being whacked enthusiastically with my own wallet
by a woman I didn't know, all in the interest of removing an allegedly
large insect that I had never seen.

Well.

After a series of authoritative swats from the stranger, the cricket /
large moth / demon-insect hopped off my back and onto the window,
and after I took a long look at it, I told Mariel I thought I might be
ready to look for an indoor table again.

And as the woman/exterminator ambled nonchalantly across the
patio to gather her things, that is exactly what we did.

Basically, you know, it was a pretty typical Friday.

Quite frankly I have no idea if the bug was a cricket or not—I am
not well-versed in insectery—but regardless of its genus and/or spe-
cies, I think about that morning all the time. And when I ponder that
whole bizarro situation, I'm convinced it's when Bright Blue and I took
our relationship to a whole new level. Like any good friend, my wallet was practical and colorful. It was fun to hang out with her. When
someone would give her a compliment, I would nod in agreement. I
was proud of her.

But on the morning we met Big Cricket Demon Bug, Bright Blue stood up for me. She protected me. She literally knocked danger off my shoulder, and yes, I realize that "danger" is way too strong a word, but just stay with me. Because between a giant insect and a stranger who felt the need to address what was happening on my person, Bright Blue was a buffer.

She got 'er done. And sure, All The Hitting was a little uncomfortable, but in that particular case, it was necessary. I mean, far be it for me to be overly dramatic, but Y'ALL I COULD HAVE DIED.

MY WALLET SAVED MY LIFE.

I really am laughing. But I'm also well aware that as much as this season of life has taught me the importance of standing up for what matters most, it has also shown me the peace and comfort that come from having a friend who will stand up for you and with you to fight the battle at hand.

Even if that friend is a wallet.

And the battle is against a genetic freak of an insect.

METAPHORS CAN BE STRANGE, OKAY?

But true story: if my inanimate wallet was able to stand strong in a time of need, then I'm optimistic that all of us human people with opposable thumbs can do a better job of standing up and looking out for each other. We might even be able to swat away someone's potential threats.

Just a little something to think about.

Who knew that Bright Blue would have so much to teach us?

CHAPTER 4

His Name Is John

At the beginning of last summer I decided to read the Gospels. After watching the nation lose its collective mind during an election—and with what some people refer to as "outrage culture" in full force on social media and cable news—I had grown tired of all the shouting and wanted to see Jesus in action on the pages of Scripture. It's a strange time to be alive in so many ways, and it feels like no matter where we land on the political spectrum, we have all been madder than a wet hen for the better part of three years. We've become a bunch of preschoolers who are stomping around Twitter and Facebook and message boards, throwing our Legos and packing up our toys and screaming at all the other kids that we don't want to play with them anymore. For these reasons and so many others, I needed to remind myself what mattered most to Jesus. I needed to pay attention to how He addressed injustice, how He treated people, how He walked and talked and ministered on this earth.

Before I could get to the Jesus-in-action parts of the Gospels, though, I needed to read through the events that happened before He was born. And I'll be honest: when it was time for me to read Luke 1, I almost skipped it. After writing a book a few years ago that focused on what transpired between Mary and Elizabeth in Luke 1, I thought I had a pretty good understanding of how that whole thing played out. But then I decided I was being ridiculous (and arrogant) (and dumb), and I opened my Bible to Luke 1. Sure enough, something jumped out that was brand-new to me.

First, some background: at a point when I am at peace with how the Lord has led me to this particular place in my life, I can still give in to the temptation to fall all over myself trying to explain and justify and appease a person who questions me. But last summer, on the morning when I read Luke 1, I was so encouraged by verses 57–66 that I sat straight up in my chair and pushed my shoulders back.

Here's the passage:

> *Now the time had come for Elizabeth to give birth, and she had a son. Then her neighbors and relatives heard that the Lord had shown her his great mercy, and they rejoiced with her.*
>
> *When they came to circumcise the child on the eighth day, they were going to name him Zechariah, after his father. But his mother responded, "No. He will be called John."*
>
> *Then they said to her, "None of your relatives has that name." So they motioned to his father to find out what he wanted him to be called. He asked for a writing tablet and wrote: "His name is John." And they were all amazed. Immediately his mouth was opened and his tongue set free, and he began to speak, praising God. Fear came on all those who lived around them, and all these*

things were being talked about throughout the hill coun-
try of Judea. All who heard about him took it to heart,
saying, "What then will this child become?" For, indeed,
the Lord's hand was with him.

Now listen up here just a minute.

Because Elizabeth and Zechariah can teach us some things that we need to know—and maybe even help us unlearn some habits that don't serve us very well anymore.

———

For the first four decades of my life—and please try to squelch any envy you may feel as a result of my personal achievements—I was an exceptional people pleaser. Sure, I liked to think that I was just super nice and quick to defer to the wants / wishes / plans of others, but the barebones reality is that what motivated me more often than not was a whole bunch of fear about what would happen if I stood up for what I believed, offered an unpopular opinion, or—my personal worst-case scenario—disappointed someone.

We could probably sit down together and figure out the thousands of reasons why this behavior was my go-to for four decades, starting with the fact that I'm the youngest child in my family by ten years and wrapping up our analysis with where I land on the various and sundry personality profiles (INFP, Enneagram 9, Sanguine/Phlegmatic, and Bingo was his name-o). Regardless of the reasons, however, there's no denying that I spent decades of my life doing my level best to leave most boats unrocked and most pots unstirred. There was still rebellion and dissension, of course, but people pleasers become experts at bury-ing that stuff where no one can see it. So in situations where I could easily skate on the surface, I was committed to keeping the people happy, my friends.

However, believing that you have to keep people happy in order to stay in their good graces is exhausting, and by the time I was in junior high, I had learned all sorts of people-pleasing quick-tricks to eliminate disagreements and tensions and conflicts. I knew how to ask questions that my teachers would like, how to add to or subtract from my personality to make social situations easier, how to be a non-confrontational listener, and how to smile politely even when I thought what someone was saying was a pile of hot garbage. I rarely challenged anyone, rarely called anyone out, and rarely said what I was actually thinking.

For the record, when I'm around people who *do* challenge and call out and say what's on their minds?

I am drawn to them like a magnet.

I see you, David Hudson.

If there had been some way you could have examined my younger self's people-pleasing skills under a microscope, you would have also discovered a deep fear of being misunderstood. If someone didn't agree with me, I needed for them to understand all the reasons why I did what I did, and if that meant I needed to share seventy-five bullet points that led me to my decision, then I was happy to oblige. Sure, someone being mad at me was awful, but it was equally terrible if someone misread my motives or didn't understand the backstory.

This is why a people pleaser's favorite accomplice is oftentimes the fine art of overexplaining.

Case in point.

I've never been more aware of how much I wanted to keep everybody happy—and keep everybody happy with me—than when Alex was about five months old and I was getting ready to go back to work.

If people began to broach the question of why I was still going to teach as opposed to staying home, I couldn't just have a normal conversation about it; I was way too fearful of disapproval. So what I would do instead was to start talking really fast about how it was going to be the best of both worlds because David worked from home and we were going to arrange our schedules so that David did most of his work in the afternoon or at night and that way Alex wouldn't have to go to daycare and actually it was going to be such a great thing for all of us because I'm actually more productive when I'm working and I love the interaction with my students and David was going to do such a good job taking care of Alex and I wasn't worried about leaving him at all because remember this is going to be the best of both worlds I think I already told you about that earlier but it's worth repeating because best of both worlds best of both worlds best of both worlds.

Raise your hand if you're now too tired to live.

Here's what I wish I had said: "I'm going back to work because I want to go back to work. Thank you for your interest and concern."

Back then, though, I couldn't do it. I couldn't rest in the short and sweet. Plus, I thought my super please-y pattern of behavior was serving me well, when the reality was that it required an insane amount of mental energy, overthinking, plate-spinning, and accommodation. What I know now is that over time, that kind of living will wear you right on down. It becomes difficult to assert what you really believe because you're not all that sure anymore; you've buried the core of who you are in an endless pile of polite head nods, soft smiles, overly enthusiastic reactions, and countless stifled opinions.

Or, in our current day and age, it might look more like an onslaught of emojis that communicate *oh my word that is the most hilarious thing I have ever heard and I totally agree with you and you are the very best person who has ever person'd!*

This irrational urge to keep everybody happy is especially strong in women, I think, mainly because many of us—especially Baby Boomers and Gen Xers, particularly in the South—were conditioned from an early age to ignore our actual feelings and pretend like everything was fine. We earned honorary PhDs in keeping the peace, smoothing over tension, appeasing the people around us, and minimizing our expectations—or even our whole dadgum selves—so we wouldn't ruffle someone else's feathers.

To be clear: this is a different deal than being "servant hearted" or "service oriented" or "consistently gracious."

Because you can be all of those things and still tell the truth.

But the people-pleasing—oh, let me tell you what—it often requires some big fat lies, and that, my friends, is what I like to call a no bueno situation. Instead of speaking the truth in love, we cower. We aim to please, after all. And if we feel like it's necessary, we will flat-out fake it.

Yes, I would love to hear what you think about how I'm super-focused on my career right now and not prioritizing the "right" "life-giving" things.

Sure, I'll be glad to lead that Bible study that conflicts with my middle kid's voice lessons and completely robs our family of the possibility of having dinner together on Tuesday nights.

No, I don't mind sharing my study guide with you at all; I totally understand why you haven't been able to make it to class all semester.

And on top of that, here's the real kicker: sometimes saying nothing at all is even worse—because silence that keeps us short-term comfortable can make us long-term complicit. So we don't confront a family member's racist comments, or we don't speak up when a friend's husband makes degrading remarks about women, or we don't challenge a coworker who's manipulating us to get what he wants.

We just go along to get along. We do our best to lay low and keep quiet and pray we don't rock the proverbial boat.

When you stand back and think about it, it's pretty cowardly.

Over the last ten or so years, thankfully, I've depended less on my people-pleasing powers and have been much better about setting and keeping boundaries. Maybe it's my age, or maybe it's that taking care of my family and my work / writing responsibilities leaves me little time to manage (much less coddle) other people's opinions and perceptions. Gradually—and I would say mercifully—I've become much more of a straight shooter. I can honestly say that at this stage of my life, I want my "yes" to be "yes," I want my "no" to be "no," and I don't care to labor under a lot of false guilt that makes me feel like I owe someone an explanation for either one of those answers.

Don't get me wrong: I want to be sacrificial and sensitive to the places where God is telling me to say yes when I want to say no. I want to be kind, too. Absolutely. But I'm learning the distinction between kindness and people-pleasing. Genuine kindness flows from love, while people-pleasing flows from fear, selfishness, and self-preservation.

I've lived that people-pleasing life. It doesn't hold nearly as much appeal as it used to.

Even still, old habits die hard. Every so often I'll be so afraid that I've disappointed someone—or that they've misunderstood me—that I almost feel like I can't breathe. It's ridiculous.

It's also a terrible way to live.

And I've had enough of it.

I really have.

Elizabeth and Zechariah had waited a long time for their baby. They had wanted to be parents for many years, and finally, one day when Zechariah was at work in the temple, an angel named Gabriel showed up and announced that Elizabeth was going to get pregnant, and that baby would be very special indeed. You can find this whole story in Luke 1:8–25, but in case you don't read the backstory, know that Elizabeth's pregnancy was a very big deal. In fact, the announcement of her pregnancy was the first time anyone had heard a peep from God or His messengers in about four hundred years. Elizabeth's baby would be the fulfillment of Malachi's prophecy at the end of the Old Testament.

Elizabeth's baby would be confirmation that God was still at work among His people.

Also, I feel like I need to mention that Elizabeth was in her sixties when she got pregnant.

(Won't He do it!)

(But maybe don't do that in me, Lord!)

Fast-forward to the circumcision in verse 59.

Elizabeth was eight days post-partum (and post-partum in her sixties, which sounds like it could either be a really good thing or a really bad thing) when it was time to circumcise her baby. The folks who showed up for the ceremony were her friends and family, and they expected that she would name her child after his father.

Elizabeth didn't budge from the plan, however: "No, he shall be called John."

I imagine that Elizabeth was sitting down when she said it. But make no mistake: figuratively and symbolically, sister was standing up.

Even still, her refusal wasn't enough for her friends and family; they meant business about questioning her decision not to have a Zechariah, Jr. So they did the exact same thing that people will do to us right here, right now, in the twenty-first century in the United States of America: they tried to go over her head. They looked to her husband and hoped to get a different answer. *Mom's not cooperating, so let's go see what Dad says.* Keep in mind that Zechariah couldn't even speak because Gabriel made him mute earlier in Luke 1 when he questioned the news about Elizabeth's upcoming pregnancy. *Still, maybe Dad can pull some silent strings or something.*

So Zechariah got out a pen and paper (okay, maybe it was a quill and a scroll, but whatever) and made his point clear: "His name is John."

Y'all. That whole exchange fires me all the way up.

Because here's the deal: Elizabeth and Zechariah's insistence on naming their baby John might not have made a lick of sense to their neighbors—however well-intentioned they were—but Elizabeth and Zechariah knew the whole story. They knew what Gabriel had said (specifically, "you shall call his name John"). They knew what the Lord had done. And even though their neighbors questioned them, they didn't talk non-stop (unlike, you know, me) for fifteen minutes in an attempt to make everybody else okay with what they were doing. HIS NAME IS JOHN.

Here's something else that occured to me. The people who questioned the decision to name the baby John—those people weren't Elizabeth and Zechariah's enemies. They were their friends. They were family. Nobody flew off the handle or screamed "HIS NAME IS JOHN" as they slammed the back door. Elizabeth and Zechariah were firm in their responses, but they weren't unkind. They certainly weren't defensive. We can all file this away for the next time we're tempted to share our thoughts in the comments section of a news story about a controversial court case or we find ourselves on the receiving end of some pointed questions at lunch with our extended family.

Granted, it's easy to forget, especially when conversations get heated, but disagreeing with someone does not make them our enemy. Disagreement also doesn't mean that in order to keep the other person happy, we have to cave like a souffle that's come out of the oven too soon. We can disagree *and* we can love one another. How about that.

And really, even though there was some disagreement, the whole exchange at John's circumcision is about so much more than a baby's name. Because after Elizabeth and Zechariah stood firm in obedience—trusting what God revealed to them through Gabriel— Zechariah was free to speak again. He didn't apologize and tell everybody how sorry he was that they didn't explain everything earlier and see this angel named Gabriel had told him how this whole thing was going to go down and blah blah blahbity blah.

Instead? He blessed God. And because of the way Elizabeth and Zechariah responded, news about John spread throughout the hill country. Don't miss this: God had been silent for four hundred years. *People needed to know this news.* And as people heard about this very special baby, they knew "that the hand of the Lord was with him." The parents' obedience gave credibility to the calling God had placed on the life of their son.

I'm gonna sit here for just a minute and read that last sentence over and over again.

So here's my encouragement to all of us: when we know the Lord has called us and directed us in a specific way? Stand there. That is holy ground. We don't have to explain the hows and whys and wheres to justify that we know that we know that we know. Our job is to tell the truth, to bless God, and to refuse to be swayed by fear of man. So stand there confidently. After all, He told you. He led you.

And finally, there's this: if we're more concerned with spinning around trying to assess everybody's opinions and reactions, trying to manage what the whole world thinks about us, we run the risk of losing the ground He has given us.

Don't you dare back down or back away for the sake of someone else's approval or in the interest of someone else's comfort with your decision.

He's already told you what to do.

His name is John.

Stand.

CHAPTER 5

Whole and Free

It's odd, looking back, that I knew.

I didn't know that I knew, of course. We rarely do. But when it came time to figure out what to do for the launch of my third book, I felt an odd conviction that I shouldn't hit the road for a bunch of promotion-y stuff. I didn't want to schedule book signings in different cities, nor did I want to try to drum up some far-flung speaking engagements.

Normally I like to travel, like to go new places, all of that. But when people would ask what I was planning for the new book's release, here's what I found myself saying, in one form or another, over and over again:

I really want to be with my family this summer. I feel like it's where I need to be.

So when book release day rolled around, all I had to do was drive from Nashville, where I had been recording some videos for the book, to my house in Birmingham. Then we probably did something totally wild and crazy and went to Chuy's to celebrate.

To be clear, we will go to Chuy's to celebrate an exciting piece of mail. So I feel like even if we didn't welcome the new book with a whole lot of fanfare, we commemorated it with some quality Mexican cuisine.

Even though it's my nature to overthink pretty much everything, I felt really good about the summertime plan. I was speaking at a couple of churches, but for the most part, the calendar was wide open. My mama had been diagnosed with dementia about eighteen months earlier, and while her memory hadn't suffered much, her speech was increasingly slow. It was hard for her to find her words, hard for her to follow through with any sort of process, and to add insult to injury, she had a toe amputated toward the end of the previous year. She worked with a physical therapist to regain her mobility; plus, my sweet friend Emma Kate, an occupational therapist, drove to my hometown one afternoon to help Mama gain some confidence with her everyday tasks. Mama adored Emma Kate, so she hung on her every word and followed her instructions to the letter.

We were so proud of how Mama worked to get stronger, but still, she struggled. There were several times when I helped her change her socks, and after she stared at her foot for a few seconds, she slowly said, "Sophie? I miss my toe." And of course she did. Anybody would. The toe situation made balance more difficult, so she needed a walker that she hated using. Sister even went to the medical supply store and got Mama a hot pink walker with flowers on it, and while that helped, Mama liked to think that she could move around without it. Every time Sister, who lives in Nashville, and I would talk on the phone, one of us would worry out loud that Mama was going to fall.

In addition, Mama's anxiety seemed to ramp up at night. We learned that the elevated frustration and fear isn't uncommon for dementia and Alzheimer's patients, but it was always heartbreaking to see Mama so out of sorts. One weekend, in fact, I was at Mama and Daddy's house, and the closer it got to Mama's bedtime, the more agitated she became. I was trying to stay calm, trying to reassure her, but it was obvious that I was getting on her nerves. When I finally got Mama into her bed—when I pulled up the covers around her and reminded her one last time that she was going to be fine—she sighed dramatically, turned her head, and said, "I'll be SO GLAD when you GO HOME."

I couldn't help but laugh. Mama even grinned a little bit.

Mama's sister, Chox, was also having health struggles; she had battled cancer for several years and had recently moved into Rolling Meadows, an assisted living facility in my hometown. The fact that Mama and Chox both had bidden farewell to their driving days meant that they didn't see each other nearly as much as they used to, so when they did see one another—like when my cousin Paige hosted our family Easter lunch—they tended to size up which one of them was in worse shape.

Paige and I have laughed so many times thinking about an Easter Sunday several years ago. Paige was checking on her guests before lunch, making sure everyone was comfortable, when Mama motioned for Paige to come closer.

"Paige," Mama said, "Chox's color is not good."

Meanwhile, Chox had found me in the kitchen and said, "Soap, Ouida is having *such* a hard time."

It was sort of like a competition no one wanted to win.

They loved one another fiercely. But there were a few long-running strands of their sibling rivalry that flat-out went the distance.

Fortunately, Mama had a phenomenal caretaker in Daddy (as did Chox in Paige), but Daddy needed a break every once in a while. This is the sort of stuff you have to start navigating anywhere north of thirty years old—aging parents, along with all the love and compassion and logistics and sadness and overwhelm and even humor that comes with them.

So the book took a backseat to what mattered more, and the plan was to keep summer open and spend as much time with Mama and Daddy as possible.

I knew it was the right thing.

Even if I couldn't have known.

The day after the book came out, Alex and I went to my hometown in Mississippi. My sole *Giddy Up, Eunice* book signing was going to be at a family friend's clothing store downtown, and when Chox had asked me a few weeks earlier if I would "give a talk" for her and her friends at Rolling Meadows, I said yes. Alex and I mainly wanted to hang out with family—Sister was going to be there, too—and Daddy had been asking us for months if we would please go to the Sims family reunion that weekend.

This is basically the marketing strategy for most *New York Times* Best Sellers. Local clothing store. Assisted living facility. Family reunion. Top of the charts.

I'm grinning.

My mother-in-law, Martha, went to Rolling Meadows with me early Thursday morning. For several years Martha has played Bingo there at least once a week—it's a good way for her to spend time with friends who have moved there—so she was thrilled to get to see her buddies and check on how everyone was doing. I had never spoken to a group where the average age was somewhere around eighty-five, but let me assure you that it was *delightful*. We had the best time (well, *I* had the best time, at least, and I hope the ladies did, too).

It wasn't long after Rolling Meadows when Alex and I went to The Liberty Shop for the book signing. Sister and Mama came in a separate car, and it was clear from the time Mama stepped through the doors that she was having a hard day. Finding her words was giving her fits, so Sister helped her find a place to sit where she would have a good view of who was there without being in the middle of conversations. There wasn't a huge crowd, but it was steady—former teachers, childhood neighbors, friends of Mama, Daddy, and Martha—and Sister and I had a ball getting to catch up with folks we don't see nearly enough. People were incredibly sweet to Mama—so understanding about her challenges—and at one point, after one of Daddy's former coworker's sat with Mama for several minutes, rubbing her hand and reminding her how much she loved her, Mama looked at Sister with sadness and frustration in her eyes. It took some time for her to find her words.

"I wish I could talk," she said.

We did, too.

It was a wonderful afternoon, but I missed hearing Mama's voice, the way she inflected "Well, heeeeeey sweet girl!" when she saw someone she loved. I missed the sound of her laugh, which was more like a melody that started at high C and then glided down an octave, usually ending with a "whew" or a "shew" or a little bit of a wheeze.

It was such a paradox: being happy and grateful that Mama was with us—and missing her, all at the same time.

Daddy and Alex left early Saturday morning so they could drive to south Mississippi and set up for the family reunion. Sister, Mama, and I were running a couple of hours behind them, but by 11:00 a.m., we were buckled in Sister's SUV and on our way. We weren't even a block from Mama and Daddy's house when Mama said, "I wish your Daddy would buy me a car like this."

Sister and I couldn't help but laugh. For one thing, Mama's driving days had been over since about a year and a half prior when she confessed that she sometimes parked her car at the grocery store and couldn't remember where she left it when it was time to leave. And for another thing, Mama's frustration with Daddy's car selection was a long-running theme in our family. She had wanted a Cadillac since approximately 1962, and Daddy was convinced that Cadillacs were "conspicuous consumption." Mama always said she wouldn't mind being conspicuous if she was driving a Cadillac, but it was a no-go. And on that Saturday, Sister's Honda Pilot seemed to meet all of Mama's transportation needs.

The family reunion was at city hall in Louin, Mississippi, and as someone who has attended a few outdoor family reunions in the heat of the Mississippi summer, I was mighty relieved for the blessing of the air-conditioning. When we walked in the meeting room, it was clear that the Sims family was out in full force. We found a place to sit down, and while Mama and Sister visited, I headed to the back of the room to "make plates." A bounty of Southern delicacies weighed down the folding tables along the back wall; as Mama would have said, there was more food than you could shake a stick at. Fried chicken, macaroni and cheese, potato salad, cornbread, barbecue chicken, roast, butterbeans, purple hull peas, seven-layer salad—not to mention one table that offered every conceivable variety of deviled egg.

After we ate our lunch, Sister asked Mama if she would like some dessert. "YES," she answered, and a few minutes later, when Sister set what can best be described as a sampler platter in front of Mama, there was no containing Mama's enthusiasm. Sugar was her love language, and based on the dessert tables, the Sims family spoke it fluently. There were cobblers and coconut pies and pound cakes and brownies—pretty much every confection imaginable short of setting a five-pound bag of sugar on the table and yelling, "Have at it." Mama's eyes danced when she saw her good dessert fortune, and she didn't just eat every bite. She scraped her plate clean.

One of Daddy's cousins presented a program on a movie that had recently been filmed in the area, and Daddy honored the family members who had passed away the previous year with a slide show. Eventually we made our way out to the car, and as she was backing out of the parking lot, Sister said, "Mama? Do you want to go to Moss Rose?"

"YES," Mama answered. So off we went.

Moss Rose is where Mama grew up, the place where she and Sister lived for a couple of years when Daddy was serving overseas. It's a place that makes Sister, Paige, and me irrationally sentimental, and every bit of that is to the credit of Lucy and John Robert Davis, our grandparents. Moss Rose isn't even a one stoplight town—there's just a blinking caution light at the intersection where a gas station used to be—but it was the center of the world to us when we were growing up. We spent countless Sunday afternoons and lazy summer days at Mamaw and Papaw's farm, where we'd drive Papaw's truck or ride on the back of the tractor or play hide and seek in the chicken house. I try not to over-romanticize it, but so much of what I understand about family is an offshoot of the roots Mamaw and Papaw put down on Highway 18 in Moss Rose.

We drove for a half hour or so—stopping at Sonic for cherry lime-ades—and when we finally hit the Moss Rose city limits, Sister's first stop was the Methodist church. We had barely pulled in the parking lot when Mama pointed at the building.

"That," she said, "is where your daddy and I married."

Tears flooded my eyes. Because yes. It's where Mama and Daddy married. It's also where she was baptized, where she rarely missed a Sunday growing up, and where one of my earliest memories is being at a dinner on the grounds, running through the grass with a chicken drumstick in my hand.

Listen. In small Southern churches, the ministry of fried chicken has its own committee.

Moss Rose Methodist is also where Mamaw and Papaw would have married on January 31, 1931 if the preacher hadn't been run-ning late. Since the preacher's tardiness made Papaw worried that he wouldn't be able to marry Mamaw that very day—and he had no intention of waiting—he took matters into his own hands. He and Mamaw jumped in the car (Sister likes to think it was a buggy, so run with that image if it strikes your fancy) and drove up the road toward the preacher's house. They met him somewhere along the way to Moss Rose, pulled over on the shoulder, and married right then and there.

On the side of the road.

In Mississippi.

In January.

It's totally fine if you think that's the best wedding story you've ever heard.

I am prone to agree.

Mama, Sister, and I left the church, turned on Highway 18, and started traveling in the direction of the cemetery. Mama was having a much better day than she did at the book signing, and as Sister drove,

Mama started to find her words. For reasons I cannot even explain, I pulled out my phone and videoed Mama as she talked—something I had never done before. But Mama was in her element, and there was no way to predict when she would be there again.

Mama mentioned that she wanted to see Mamaw and Papaw's gravesite, so Sister pulled in the cemetery. She helped Mama out of the car while I got Mama's walker out of the back, and with one of us on each side, we guided Mama up the hill. The ground was rocky, and though she didn't exactly have all-terrain tires on her walker, she made it. We talked for several minutes as we stood there, trying to ignore the dark gray cloud that was looming like a mountain behind us. Eventually the possibility of having to get Mama down the hill in a rainstorm convinced us to get back to the car.

As it turned out, the rain held off, so Sister drove down to Mamaw and Papaw Davis's old farm. My orthopedic boot (I had taken a tumble at the SEC baseball tournament a few weeks before) meant climbing the fence was off-limits, but Sister was all about it. As Mama and I watched, she hopped over the rails in her skinny jeans, kimono, and wedges just like the stylish trespasser we would all hope to be. Sister walked around for a few minutes, took a whole bunch of pictures, then hopped back over the fence and jumped in the car just as the rain started to fall. She showed Mama pictures of the old smokehouse, the cattle gap, and the chicken house, and after she put up her phone and started to drive again, she asked Mama if she would like to see the back part of the land.

"YES," Mama answered.

Within seconds Sister turned down a little side road that runs around the perimeter of the property, and Mama started to talk again. She pointed out the place where her childhood home used to stand— before Papaw built "the new house"—and she reminisced about life on the farm. When we got to a point where we could see the ponds Papaw used to fish, Sister stopped the car.

We took in the scenery for a bit before we looped back to the highway and headed home.

It was one of our very best days.

Two weeks later, Sister called just as the sun was coming up. I was in Tupelo, Mississippi, after speaking at a church there the night before.

I knew, even though I didn't know: something had happened to Mama.

Sister didn't have all the details, but Mama had gotten Daddy up in the night to tell him that she was having trouble catching her breath. He called an ambulance, and by the time the EMTs got to the house, Mama had stopped breathing. They resuscitated her after they got to the hospital, but she went without oxygen for a long time.

"She's in ICU," Sister said.

I was already packing my bag.

I don't have any idea how much time passed—maybe it was twenty minutes, maybe it was an hour—but I called David, threw on some clothes, and texted a few friends to ask for prayer. I checked out of the hotel, grabbed some coffee, and made a beeline for Highway 45. When I called Sister to let her know that I was on the road, I asked her to repeat what she knew. I was more awake by that point—caffeine was helpful in that process—and as she went over what had happened, I started to understand how serious Mama's condition was. I told Sister I would update her and Brother as soon as I got to the hospital. They were in Nashville and Memphis—not quite as close as I was—so it was going to take them longer to get there. Plus, we weren't exactly sure what the situation was going to be when I finally got to the hospital.

I couldn't figure out what to listen to as a drove—podcasts and news felt like way too many words, and music on the radio seemed weird, somehow. Out of nowhere I remembered an album our friend Travis recorded about ten years ago. Travis is a dear friend to David and me, so I knew it would be comforting to listen to his voice, and there was one song in particular I wanted to hear. I pulled it up on my phone, and I bet I listened to it twenty times over the next two hours. I just kept going back to it, over and over. The lyrics were a balm to my heart because they pointed me straight to Psalm 145:

> *One generation commends your works to another . . .*
> *They speak of the glorious splendor of your majesty . . .*
> *They tell of the power of your awesome works . . .*
> *They celebrate your abundant goodness*
> *and joyfully sing of your righteousness.*
> *I will exalt you, my God the King . . .*
> *My mouth will speak in praise of the Lord . . .*
> *Let every creature praise his holy name*
>   *for ever and ever.*
> *(vv. 4a, 5a, 6a, 7, 1a, 21 NIV)*

It was mid-morning when I got to the hospital, and if I had any lingering resistance to the idea that Mama's condition was serious, the number of people surrounding Daddy in the ICU waiting room would have cured me of it. I was shocked, honestly, by how many friends and relatives were there, and I was also deeply grateful that Daddy hadn't been alone. I hugged him before I spoke to anyone else, and while he hadn't been back to sleep since Mama woke him in the middle of the night, he seemed to be holding up pretty well. He said we'd go back to see Mama in just a few minutes, and as he turned to say goodbye to a friend who had stopped by, Mama's cousin Judy grabbed my arm and pulled me close. I will never forget the kindness in her eyes as she started to speak.

"I want you to be prepared," she said, "for what you're going to see. She's not herself. So just know that before you go back there."

She hugged my neck and told me she loved me before I walked away with Daddy. Normally Chox would step in as a surrogate mama in situations like that, but Chox was actually in the same hospital, three floors up, recovering from surgery to repair a broken hip. Only the Lord could tell us how she and Mama managed to wind up in the same hospital at the same time, but I feel certain that if they had any say in the matter, they would have found some time to meet up on a neutral floor and assess how the other one was doing.

God love 'em.

Daddy and I walked over to ICU and waited for someone to let us in the door. He led me back to Mama's bed, and it didn't take long to realize that Mama was struggling. I don't think there's any need to get into the specifics of that, but the nurse very sweetly explained a couple of things about Mama's condition that I didn't understand. After several minutes of talking through the nurse's answers with Daddy, he kissed Mama's cheek and asked if I wanted to stay with Mama a little while longer.

I did.

After Daddy left, I walked over to the far side of the bed, grabbed Mama's hand, and said the same words over and over.

"Oh, Mama. You're having such a hard time."

I stood there for fifteen or twenty minutes, not saying much, just watching Mama, eavesdropping on chatter from the nurse's station, listening to the rhythm of the machines beside Mama's bed.

Trying to make sense of it all.

I knew I needed to go back to the waiting room, to call Sister and Brother, to check on Daddy, to talk to the doctor. And while I had no idea if Mama could hear me or not, I wanted to make sure to say it:

"Mama, He holds you in the palm of His hand."
"He holds you in the palm of His hand."
"He holds you in the palm of His hand."

The next two days were a blur. There was no change in Mama's condition, and we spent most of our time at the hospital. I know that so many people have been in similar situations; after all, no family escapes illness, trauma, or grief, so our family's experience wasn't unique. In fact, it's pretty common. What varies, I think, from family to family and situation to situation, is where comfort comes from—or if we're willing to let ourselves be comforted at all.

Mama would never have believed it, but she was actually a huge source of comfort for us. Sister had only been in town a few hours when she discovered Mama's prayer journal in a dresser drawer, and late at night or early in the mornings, we would flip through the journal, amazed by how Mama had covered those pages in her handwriting over the years. We read through her prayer lists, her thoughts about Scripture, and her written prayers. Between the verses Mama had underlined in her Bible and the thousands of words she had written in her journal, she continued to mother us, continued to shepherd us, and continued to remind us of a perspective much bigger than our circumstances. Mama's words were an unexpected gift, an unexpected source of peace.

"Only a true, loving God," she wrote, "could give me the peace and serenity I feel when I am troubled or when others are troubled. God is always there for each one of us. If we would only seek His presence and guidance daily—we would know that He is a God of *mercy*. His Love is *bigger* than *any problem we have*."

Yes, ma'am.

And listen—if I have a hundred more years, I will never get over the countless ways the body of Christ cared for us while Mama was in ICU. Those days were as surreal as anything I've experienced in my adult life, but the consistent presence of God's people was comforting, life-giving, and healing.

There was Mama and Daddy's pastor—who listened to us, prayed with us, prayed over Mama, and guided us so compassionately as we navigated unfamiliar territory.

There were nurses and doctors—who answered questions, cared for Mama so tenderly, and met us many times a day with great compassion.

There were friends and family—who anticipated what we needed before we even knew we needed it, provided meals, and showed up over and over again. Some people brought casseroles, some people brought books, and some people sat with us in silence. The ministry of presence is a real thing. We are forever grateful for those ministers.

There was Daddy—devastated, steady as the sun, unwavering in his love for his bride and his commitment to his family.

There was Jesus. Our very present Help. Our Hope. Our Comforter.

Thanks be to God.

On Monday, the neurologist told us that Mama's condition was the result of a massive stroke. Her left side was completely paralyzed, which helped us understand why she hadn't moved during her time in the hospital, why her head stayed stationary against her left shoulder, why her chin had been buried against the left side of her chest. He went on to communicate concerns about Mama's brain activity, and when we walked away from our conversation with him, we understood that while Mama would be healed, she would not be healed this side of heaven.

I can't speak for the group, of course, but I felt the strangest sense of calm after we heard the doctor's news. We said many times over the weekend that we wanted Mama to be whole and free, and if you've walked with the Lord a little while, you know that we don't necessarily get to set the terms for how that's going to look.

The doctor gave us a time line of hours, not days, and Sister, Brother, and I wanted to stay with Mama. So did Paige, who had always been Mama's temperament twin, more of a third daughter than a niece. Daddy said he didn't think he could watch Mama take her last breath—a decision we understood and respected—so, after Mama and Daddy's pastor prayed with all of us around Mama's bed, Daddy held down the fort in the waiting area, and "the children," as Mama liked to call us, kept vigil back in ICU.

At first Sister, Brother, and I were the only three people with Mama; Paige, who had been running back and forth between Chox's room and Mama's cubby (area? room-ette? I'm unfamiliar with ICU terminology) for the better part of four days, was somehow still standing and heading our way after she took care of a few things for Chox. Brother had stopped at the coffee shop before he went into ICU, and unbeknownst to us, he bought a bunch of sandwiches in case anybody wanted a snack.

For the longest time, it seemed, Sister stood at the top of the bed on one side, I stood at the top of the bed on the other side, Brother stood beside me at the foot of the bed, and we reminisced about the most random things. We talked to Mama even though she couldn't answer us, and we laughed as much as we cried. After a half hour or so, Brother piped up and said, "Hey—I have some sandwiches over there if anybody wants one."

Sister and I politely declined, but the third time he asked—"Does anybody want a sandwich?"—Sister laid it out.

"We are not eating sandwiches around Mama's bed! She would not have it!"

Y'all. The three of us got so tickled. Because Mama *really* would not have had it. Not for a minute. There's a time and a place to set up a makeshift buffet, but that wasn't it. It occurred to me, though, that Brother was just doing what Mama had always done: trying to make everybody more comfortable when life was hard. There was something really sweet about that.

It wasn't much later when Mama's friends / surrogate children the Haleses came in to say their good-byes. Mama would have been so grateful; she had loved their family for almost thirty years, and they had loved her so beautifully in return. Paige's brother, Benji, also stopped by, which would have made Mama smile; she still called him "mischievous" even though he was fifty years old.

Paige walked in not too long after Benji left, and she took up the spot across from Brother. We didn't say much, but every once in awhile I would look over at Paige and see giant tears falling from her eyes straight onto the sheet at the end of the bed. They didn't even roll down her cheek; they just watered the space around Mama's feet.

A small window in the corner of Mama's room let us know that a summer thunderstorm was coming, and from time to time my orthopedic boot and I would hobble over and look outside. A near-black cloud hung heavy above the street in front of us, while off to the left, shards of light were working like crazy to escape the darkness. The rain finally came late in the afternoon, and it was loud and relentless, hitting the window from two different angles, it seemed. In the strangest way, it was perfect. Mama had always loved a good summer storm.

It was early in the evening when I sat down to rest my foot while Sister, Brother, and Paige continued to stand around the bed. Brother was keeping an eye on Mama's heart rate, which had dropped significantly over the course of the afternoon. I pulled out my phone to text David a quick update, but before I hit "send," Paige broke the silence.

"She's not breathing," she said. "She's stopped breathing."

I hopped up and took an awkward step toward the bed. The four of us stood at what I had come to think of as our posts, all of us looking at Mama, then at the monitor, then at Mama, then at the monitor.

"It's okay, Mama," Sister whispered. "It's okay."

About that time, the monitor started to beep, confirmation that, as Paige had said, Mama was no longer breathing. All four of us had a hand on Mama, all four of us still as stones, deep in our thoughts and memories as we settled into the reality of what was happening.

Maybe that's why what happened next was so shocking, so stunning—and why I would swear I had made it up if three other people hadn't been in the room with me.

As the monitor's beeping drowned out every other noise around us, Mama's head began to lift off of her shoulder just like it was on a string. The motion was slow, controlled, graceful—as the four of us stood, wide-eyed, stunned, not sure what to make of what we were seeing.

Brother spoke up first: "She's moving," he said. "She's moving."

Mama's wasn't breathing. But her head continued to move up, and up, and up for several more seconds until it was centered, squared with her body, pointed straight ahead—after days of being almost folded into her shoulder. The movement paused before her head reclined just the slightest bit and rested against her pillow.

She looked thirty years younger than she had even a minute before. All the stress and strain we had seen on her face—the places that had clearly been affected by her stroke—every bit of that was gone.

That hospital room was holy ground.

We will never get over it.

About that time Mama's nurse walked in, and when I looked at her, I was slack-jawed.

"That," I said, with maybe too much enthusiasm, "That was beautiful. That was the most beautiful thing I've ever seen!"

Paige, of course, had a full-on waterfall running down her face. Sister kept staring at Mama, then shaking her head—like she couldn't believe what she just saw. Brother was in a similar state.

And y'all, several minutes later, when we walked out of the ICU to tell Daddy and our family and friends that Mama was in heaven, I must have looked like I had won a game show. It was the complete opposite of any reaction I ever thought I would have—losing Mama had always been my greatest fear—but I made a beeline for Alex Hudson, grabbed his thirteen-year-old face, and looked straight in his eyes.

"We are going to be sad," I said. "And we are going to miss her. But I want you to hear me say this: We can be so happy for her. We can be SO HAPPY for her."

We sat with our people for maybe a half hour, crying and laughing and figuring out what we needed to do next.

All of that I expected.

But what I didn't expect?

The rejoicing.

Later that night, I laid in bed at Mama and Daddy's house, utterly incapable of finding sleep no matter how hard I chased it. David had gone back to Birmingham to get funeral clothes, so I was the only one in the room, and after tossing and turning for who knows how long, I turned on the light and sat up on the edge of the bed.

Lord, why did we get to see that? I wondered.

Lord, what was that? What exactly did we see?

I grabbed my phone off the nightstand and opened up my browser. Since I couldn't seem to make sense of it all, I decided to turn to Google.

As you do.

Here's what I typed. No lie.

Do people who have massive strokes and are paralyzed on their left side lift their heads when they die?

Shockingly, Google was not helpful.

It didn't stop me from asking, though.

The next morning I sent a text to a friend of mine who's a Bible teacher I respect so much. I said, in so many words, *Hey—I just need you to know what we saw yesterday.* Then I explained what happened when Mama stopped breathing. My friend wrote me back almost immediately, and she said, in so many words, *Hey—I just need you to know that you saw Jesus take your sweet mother home.*

Later that day, Sister, Brother, and I sat in the den with Daddy while the preacher helped us plan Mama's funeral. Our conversation turned to the last few moments of Mama's life, and Brother summed it up best, I think.

"It was a miracle," he said. "It really was. A miracle."

I thought about something Mama had written in her prayer journal; Sister and I had found it just a couple of days before.

"Last week, I was ill, and God reassured me that this too shall pass. His left hand is under my head, and His right hand caresses me. God has always been my defense. His eternal arms are my support."

I don't think Mama would have been at all surprised by what we saw when she died, because she already knew it. She knew it way down deep in her bones, where Truth seeps into the marrow.

Grief, of course, came later, rolling in and out in waves, never announcing when it planned to arrive or when it would show itself the door. In so many ways, we're *still* grieving, trying as best we can to manage the gaps, to figure out what life looks like without Mama here.

We miss her. No doubt. But she continues to teach us—and that has been such a sweet source of comfort. We have our memories: so many stories, so many phrases unique to Mama, so many telling facial expressions. We have the comments in her cookbooks: *great for a dinner party!* or *this was a hit!* or *perfect for a bridesmaid's luncheon!* We have her Bible: the notes in the margins, the passages she underlined so many times that she nearly punctured the paper. We have her prayer journal: years of prayer lists, years of responses to Scripture, years of written prayers.

We have the last day of her earthly life: completely healed, completely restored, completely whole, completely free.

We grieve. Of course we do.

But we remember that even her very last breath pointed us to Jesus.

So we grieve with hope. We grieve with peace.

And we stand in that hope and peace, even when things feel shaky and sad. We trust the literal Lifter of her head.

We know he holds her in the palm of His hand.

CHAPTER 6

Done with Being Done

I've struggled with my weight my whole life.

Seriously. My WHOLE life. I can't remember a time—not one single time—when my weight / food / clothing size / general fitness level wasn't hovering in the back of my mind, an omnipresent nag that I needed to address but preferred to ignore.

I've dealt with the nag in all sorts of ways—some of them healthy, most of them not—but for the bulk of my adult life, my response to dealing with my weight was just to pretend like it wasn't an issue. Like Suzanne Sugarbaker in *Designing Women*, I would throw on an extra layer of something drape-y and flowy and call it a day. It might sound strange to most people, but my weight never really interfered with my confidence, despite the fact that internet strangers have occasionally piped up to let me know how I was failing myself.

About four years ago, though, something shifted. Physically, at least, I started to feel like I was falling apart, and I think that's because I was falling apart. My blood pressure was sky high, I had a rash on my legs that wouldn't clear up for love nor money, I was having horrible headaches (and stomachaches), and my lack of connection to or control of my body left me super frustrated. For three years my primary physical activity had been writing books—which, news flash, isn't an actual physical activity—and my sedentary lifestyle left me feeling like a bump on a log. Nothing about me was at ease in my own skin. My energy was low, my favorite hobby was sleeping, and my beverage of choice was as many Diet Cokes as I could ingest in a 24-hour period.

So, you know, things weren't great.

I knew that the whole situation had gotten away from me when I realized that I was finding ways to avoid my husband. I don't mean that I hid in the laundry room when he got home from work and then left the house until he fell asleep, but in ways both subtle and obvious, I made myself mostly unavailable to him. I'm not just talking about That Special Relationship between husband and wife—because I can look back and see that, in lots of ways, I checked out on him emotionally as well.

Here's an example.

David and I have always, throughout our marriage, sat down for thirty or forty-five minutes before suppertime and downloaded the day: work, problems, plans, funny stories, current events, whatever. And while I probably couldn't have told you why—outside of some vague sense of annoyance—I began dodging and weaving and deflecting and disengaging from our daily check-ins. I've only realized it in hindsight—I couldn't see it when I was in the middle of it—but I would tell him I was worn out from the drama of the day (I switched from a teaching job to my current Dean of Women job back in 2014, and, in fairness, it was vocational whiplash), or I would cite some sort of pressing deadline, or I would mention Some Urgent Task Requiring Great Urgency. Sometimes I would just busy myself in another part of the house and pretend like our evening routine was nonexistent.

The point was that I didn't want to engage in anything that might scratch beneath the surface, that would require me to get honest about what was going on with me way deep down. I just kept it moving and oh my word I'm so busy and yes we need to talk about that at some point but let me just go ahead and run Alex to practice and maybe we can revisit that topic down the road but really I mean never because I don't have any intention of telling you that I am borderline troubled about my physical health and I haven't worked out in about four years and I'm also super sad about all the ways my mama is struggling with her own health but it's gonna be way easier emotionally if I just work on this article I'm writing or maybe watch ninety-two Mississippi State football highlights in a row and thanks so much for being here love you bye.

So I did the practice run or worked on the book/article/blog, and around 8:30 or 9:00 every night, I "posted up" in the guest room. I fluffed up the pillows on the bed, sat back (always with my computer on my lap), and worked my way through my shows on the DVR. With the exception of *Mad Men* and *Survivor*, David and I haven't watched the same shows since about 2007, so it's not unusual for us to watch different stuff at night. But here's what I had going on back in 2015 (and, honestly, at other points in our marriage when I, for whatever reason, didn't want to been seen/known/vulnerable): I watched my shows, snuggled up with my computer and my dog, and after David would fall asleep in our room, I pulled back the covers of the guest room bed, made myself comfortable, and slept right there—with my husband across the hall.

If boundaries in our physical space mirror our degree of emotional separation—well, yes. That.

From time to time David would make a funny comment about "my" room—and Alex would even make references to "Mama's room"—but listen. I WAS NOT INTERESTED IN DIGGING

INTO THAT ISSUE. And while some happily married couples have to sleep in separate rooms for certain nights or seasons due to all sorts of stuff (personal health issues, sick kids, travel, and so on), this wasn't that. This was a whole different deal. This was me looking for places to hide because I didn't want to deal with—or come close to anyone who might pick up on—the disconnect I had created between my soul and my body.

My soul was all "I love Jesus!" and "My life is an offering!" and "Great is Thy faithfulness!" My body, on the other hand, was all "Hey. I'm not sure if you've picked up on it, but what we're trying to work with here is at a whole new level of BROKE DOWN."

In April of 2016, I went to Mississippi State's spring football game with my friend Daphne and her brother, Joel. Before the game we wanted to stop by the Cotton District Arts Festival, and while an arts festival isn't typically my go-to, I was excited about looking for a painting or photograph that might work on a gallery wall in our house. The main road was already packed with cars, so Joel, who knows every back road / side road / connecting path in Starkville, parked on a street behind the Catholic church, knowing it would just be a short walk to University Drive and all the artsy goodness. We got out of his car, walked to the end of the street, and stood in front of maybe twelve steps that led to the church's back parking lot. The steps were a little steep—nothing unreasonable, though—so Joel went first, then me, then Daph.

No big deal, right?

I'm not exaggerating when I tell you that when I got to the top of those steps, I thought, *So, is this when I finally have a heart attack?* My heart felt like it was going to race right out of my chest, and despite my best efforts to appear nonplussed by the extreme stair climbing (I promise I just rolled my eyes), I was rattled. I was winded. And I was mad.

About an hour later, after we left the Arts Festival and parked on campus for the game, I tripped on a piece of concrete as we were walking to the stadium. I fell so hard that I wondered if I had broken my kneecap, and maybe the worst part was that I was embarrassed by how difficult it was for me to get back on my feet after I fell. I spent most of the spring game nursing my hands and my left knee—I had skinned them pretty impressively—not to mention that I was nursing an ego that was bruised worse than any appendage.

Then, roughly six weeks after the spring game, I fell when I was walking into the SEC Baseball Tournament (Daph was with me again) (IS DAPH A SABOTEUR?) (I kid). We were moving pretty quickly because we wanted to claim our seats before State's game against Alabama, and about halfway down the concourse, the front of my shoe caught on the lip of a tile. I couldn't believe that I had fallen again—what are the odds, really?—and while yes, I certainly seemed to have a knack for locating tripping hazards at athletic events, the bigger issue rolling around in my head was that I was zero percent agile. It made me feel like I didn't have any control over my own body, and I wondered if I had gradually given up on ever having enough internal discipline to change.

My fall at the baseball tournament actually resulted in a broken foot, and thanks to a friend who works for the SEC, one of the trainers was able to X-ray my foot at the baseball field (true story) and put me in an orthopedic boot on site. I even stayed and watched the Bulldogs take down the Tide in a 5–1 win. That would be the silver lining, I guess. But the days after the game were a real drag; I spent the next eight weeks in a boot, hobbling around, nursing the stupid rash that wouldn't go away, feeling every bit like a foreigner in my own body.

And that was one of the most frustrating parts of the situation I had created for myself: I was uncomfortable in my own skin. Any exertion made me feel like I was wearing a padded suit, something that hindered my ability to move around without tipping over.

On top of all that, there was this: no matter where I was or what I was doing, I considered what physical activity might be required of me and bowed out when it seemed like too much. After all, I couldn't walk up a staircase without feeling like my pulse was going to beat its way out of my neck, so I dreaded putting myself in situations where I needed to navigate a bunch of stairs or walk long distances. You would have never known that any of this stuff bothered me—nobody does "breezy" better than I do, my friends—but I started sifting every outing through the filter of how difficult it might be for me physically. Were we going to have to park too far away at a concert? Would I be able to keep up with the other people in my group? Would I be able to walk fast enough to make my layover? Would we have to walk up a steep hill at one of Alex's football games?

And planning a vacation? I wasn't interested. Going to amusement parks has always been one of our family's favorite things to do together, but by 2015, there was no way I would participate in any sort of Six Flags / Universal Studios / Disneyland excursion. A theme park would require way more walking than I could manage, and since my size had officially started to make me self-conscious, I wasn't interested in throwing on shorts and a T-shirt and enjoying a day at, say, Islands of Adventure. Even my beloved beach trips caused similar dilemmas; I hated putting on a swimsuit, and I dreaded walking down to the water. Some of my very favorite memories with Alex are from the hours we've spent on the beach or in the pool, so my newly developed resistance to both roller coasters *and* the Gulf of Mexico felt like a real low.

I lived in that low place for about a year and a half.

And I pretended like everything was fine—until my mama died.

—•—

It's such a cliché, but there's nothing like the death of someone you love to make you reconsider how you're living your life. In my case I spent the days and weeks after Mama passed away contemplating the fact that something had to give—at least in terms of how I took care of myself. Because while I don't remember crying a whole lot, I definitely remember dealing with some dialed-all-the-way-up anxiety, and it scared me. I could be minding my own business—doing something super boring like cooking supper or sorting the mail—when my heart would start hammering in my chest. It was the same feeling I had after climbing those steps behind the Catholic church, only there was no physical exertion that would have prompted my heart rate to shoot up. I knew that I needed to exercise—I would even say that I *wanted* to exercise—but unless you've been in a situation where you've allowed your body or your size to spiral out of control, you have no idea how intimidating it is to try to grab hold of the reins. In fact, there are times when grabbing hold of the reins seems impossible—like there's absolutely no way it can be done.

But here was my Big Lesson of 2016: the Lord, y'all—He really can make a way. And He really does. Even in the places where we're so stuck that it feels like there's no way out.

About five months before Mama died, David and I had joined a new small group at our church (more about that later, but here's the short version). There were five families in our small group, and two of them—the Mixons and the Coonses—had daughters who went to school with Alex. We'd known each other peripherally for a long time—we had all attended the same church for years—but it was during our kids' 6th grade year when we seemed to run into one another more frequently. Since I had always worked at my high school, I didn't know many of the elementary school moms from Alex's grade, and Kasey and Stephanie helped me spread my relational wings in that regard. They became a safe place to talk about whatever was on my mind, and eventually we realized that we were all looking for a deeper sense of community right here in Birmingham.

So when I broke my foot, our small group people were super supportive. And in late July, when the boot came off and the orthopedist told me that I needed to walk on the treadmill to help with my foot rehab, they—along with David—were my cheering section.

They didn't even know, y'all. They had no idea how hard it was for me to say, "Hey, I think I'm going to start walking a little bit." If I had told them how risky that felt, they probably would have thought I was being silly. But they encouraged me, and without even knowing it, they provided the accountability I needed.

Hopefully, that's the way it goes for all of us, right? When we finally get ready to make a change—whether that's eating better or drinking less or quitting porn or mustering up the courage to throw off whatever sin has entangled us (Heb. 12:1–3)—we have people in our lives who will run with us in that direction and cheer for us every step of the way.

David had been a member at a local gym for several years, but after I made my I AM GOING TO WALK declaration, we joined one that was closer to our house (which, by the way, was a real game changer). And one summer afternoon, after years of needing to take better care of my body, I finally drove to the gym, and I finally got out of my car, and I finally stepped on a treadmill, and I finally started walking.

I didn't walk fast, and I didn't walk far. But I walked.

And despite the fact that the voice in my head had conditioned me to believe that I would owe everyone in that gym an explanation—"I APOLOGIZE THAT I AM SO OVERWEIGHT AND OUT OF SHAPE BUT YOU SEE I BROKE MY FOOT AND MY DOCTOR SUGGESTED WALKING FOR REHAB AND THIS IS VERY HARD FOR MY PRIDE NOT TO MENTION MY CALVES BUT I REALLY WANT TO DO BETTER EVERYBODY"—nobody gave me even a second glance.

I don't want to over-dramatize it, but it felt just a little bit like I was starting a revolution on behalf of my own stinkin' self.

I walked consistently for the next three or four weeks, then fell off the workout wagon after school started in August. I think this part of my tale of exercise resistance is important, because it's how lots of us roll: we make a positive change, and then we decide in all our selfish wisdom that we don't really need to be *that* consistent, that we've GOT THIS THING, that we're fine, really, IT IS ALL SO FINE.

This kind of reasoning is, of course, a giant pile of cow manure. But here's what happened during my stint off the wagon. David and Alex gave me a FitBit for my birthday, which was really helpful for me in terms of seeing in quantifiable data that 1) my resting heart rate was off the charts and 2) when I wasn't exercising, I didn't move around nearly as much as I liked to think I did. I wasn't a full-on sloth, but I probably qualified as a turtle. And then, late one night when I was doing my best to justify to David why I didn't have time to go to the gym and exercise regularly and etc., he called me on every bit of my bull. He had never said a word during the four years prior when I started getting away from myself, but I wasn't talking about making any changes back then, either. However, after I attempted to make a commitment—then tried to make a case for why making those changes just wasn't going to work out for me—he was not having it. I knew it in the back of my mind, of course, but our "spirited fellow-ship" (Christian-speak for "we had a fight") reminded me that my excuses were just excuses. They weren't actual, legitimate reasons. And if I really wanted to see changes in my health—if I really and truly wanted that—I was the only one who could make it happen.

So at the beginning of the next week (I couldn't let David win, like, the very next day), I went back to the gym, and I started walking again. Six weeks later, I thought about how strong I felt when David and I married, how much I used to love doing weight training exercises, and after my walk, I tippy-toed over to the weight room. I expected people to stare at me—to wonder what in the world I was doing on those weight machines—but you will not be surprised to learn that nobody gave a rip.

And every single time I mentioned to my friends that I went to the gym, that I was going walking, that I might try a new weight machine, their reactions—something along the lines of "GET IT, SOPH" or "YES MA'AM—you enjoy those weights!" or "good job going to the gym!"—spurred me along in ways they'll probably never understand. I had no idea how much I needed it.

I also had no idea how much working out regularly would affect the other parts of my life. When I finally committed to dealing with the physical stuff, my emotions did a 180 as well. It wasn't long at all before I stopped using the guest room as an apartment and got back in the bed with my husband.

So there's that.

A few months after I started exercising consistently, we made a Spring Break trip to Universal Studios with the Mixons and the

Coonses. Y'all, I walked all over that park—up, down, sideways, in circles—and not only that, I felt incredible (I'm grinning because it's true). And for the rest of the spring and early summer, I tried to be extra-disciplined with my exercise because Alex and I were going with Compassion International to Kenya, and Compassion will always trick you into some form of hike. I went into that trip feeling stronger than I had in a couple of decades, and about a month after we got home from Africa, David and I went to New York to celebrate our twentieth wedding anniversary.

We walked something like eighty-five thousand steps over the course of our four days exploring the city, and over and over again I thought about how even a year before, I would have been physically incapable of doing that trip. I couldn't have walked that much. I couldn't have walked that far. I couldn't have handled all the up and down on the subway stairs. When we walked across Central Park from the west side to the east side, I would have had to sit down after the first hill. And while I can't think for long about what I missed by checking out of my own life for a few years—by letting fear envelop my body, by believing the lie that I couldn't do a thing to change it—I can tell you without a second's hesitation that our New York trip was one of my favorite things I've done in my whole life. David and I had an absolute blast. We laughed like crazy and enjoyed being together like crazy and talked over and over about how a twentieth anniversary trip puts a honeymoon to shame.

But without the nudge from my husband and the encouragement of my friends—well, I would have missed that whole thing.

The Lord made a way. I'm so grateful.

It's been a little over a year since that New York trip (we went back again for our twenty-first anniversary, by the way). For sure I've navigated some lulls in my pursuit of better health, and as I always say, I am nobody's "after" picture. Even though I've lost about thirty pounds, it wouldn't make me sad to lose more, but I'm not super stressed about it because I feel pretty great—so much better than I imagined I could. Thanks to my very kind doctor and two years of consistent exercise, my heart rate doesn't warp science anymore, and my blood pressure is under control. I'm growing to love the elliptical as much as I have loved the treadmill, and I'll have you know that I have even been to Zumba. I still get in the weight room and get after it with those weights, and when I'm stressed I like to go to the park by our house and walk until the tension fades away. Occasionally I'm even fast.

And I've learned some things, too.

Last year my friend Liz told me about an exercise class called Sol Dance, and the deal with Sol Dance is that the instructor plays a (very loud) medley of popular songs—sometimes with a theme—and for one hour you dance however you feel like dancing to that music.

The catch? It is pitch-black dark in the room.

Seriously. You can't see your hand in front of your face.

The first time I went to Sol Dance, I chose a spot in a back corner of the studio. I wasn't exactly sure what to do when the lights went out; there was so much freedom that I couldn't figure out how I wanted to move. Plus, I was scared that I was going to run into the person beside me or the person in front of me, so for fifteen minutes, probably, I did some version of step-touch, step-touch, like the warm-up segment of a Jane Fonda aerobics video from back in the day.

Feel the burn, ladies.

Eventually, though, I started to move my arms and even jump a little bit. I figured out that the glow-in-the-dark floor sticker that marked my spot was my friend, because it helped me keep my bearings. It helped me understand my boundaries, it helped me know when

I moved a little too far, and on a couple of occasions, when I worked my way back into the corner, I turned around—and that little sticker showed me the way out.

It was just the tiniest bit of light, but man, was it ever effective.

The same is true with our real-life struggles, of course—whether it's our weight or a difficult relationship or a long-term addiction or a persistent anger that feels like it's going to swallow you whole. Whatever it is, it can be tricky to navigate. Sometimes we don't know which way to go. Sometimes we go too far. Sometimes we wind up in a corner and we're not entirely sure how to get out.

But when we're finally ready to move, it's good to remind ourselves that all it takes is just a little bit of light. A little bit of Light.

And I'm here to tell you this: He will do it. You can trust Him with it. Trust Him in it. Talk about it. Do the work you know you need to do. Listen to the people who love you. See how the Light starts to shine brighter and brighter.

I thought, for the longest time, that I wanted to be skinnier. But what I know now is that more than anything, I want to be strong. I want a healthier body so that I can be healthier for the Body. So that I can serve the Body.

So that I can love and stand for the Body for a really long time.

I don't know what's dark for you right now, but I do know this: light that shines from the Lord and His people can help you stand longer and stronger than you imagined. The Light will make a way in it, through it, and out of it.

Whether it's needing to take charge of your health, or your fear, or your indecision, or your need for control, or whatever, the Light is a difference maker.

Ask me how I know.

CHAPTER 7

If I May Make a Suggestion

I don't buy a whole lot of magazines these days, probably because the internet has convinced most of us that we can't be bothered with, like, *flipping pages* anymore.

GAH. It is so exhausting, the flipping. Swiping or clicking is so much more sophisticated.

I do, however, still read magazines—just on my iPad. The iPad is a dear friend of mine for lots of reasons, but one of my favorite features is that, when reading a magazine, I can pinch and zoom the text—which enables me to read without wearing reading glasses. You young things might not understand the blessing of the pinch and zoom, but that is because your eyes are still cooperative. Enjoy them while you can, my friends, and know that one day, you too will experience the joys of picking up a printed item and waiting with expectancy for your eyes to focus—only to realize that focusing is no longer a task that interests your baby blues.

So the pinch and zoom, it is wondrous. I can see the text, I can read, and I can examine the detail on Beyonce's concert cut-offs (they look like light blue denim, but they're actually quite sparkly). I have also been known to use the pinch and zoom to count JLo's abs, but it's actually not necessary because SISTER IS RIPPED and those abs are visible even when they're out of focus.

It is my great joy to provide you with this information.

Even though I rarely buy magazines, I still like to keep my eyes peeled for engaging headlines at the grocery store check-out. Many times the headlines are straight-up fiction, otherwise Jennifer Aniston would be the mother to fourteen children by now and happily reunited with Brad Pitt.

The tabloid headlines, however, aren't really what interest me. It's the women's magazines that could entertain me for the better part of an afternoon. Women's magazine headlines make some serious promises, and they're usually just believable enough that I'm tempted to put them to the test.

> *Lose 35 pounds by eating watermelon!* (Okay. I am intrigued by this premise.)
>
> *Reset your metabolism in four days!* (Is that legal? Does it require special equipment?)
>
> *Seven steps to better gut health!* (Listen. My gut will take all the help it can get. Tell me more, magazine.)

There are typically headlines about menu planning or organizing a pantry or putting the fire back in your marriage, a topic that inevitably makes me think, *Easy, magazine. People are tired, and we are no longer spring chickens. Also, have you built a fire lately? Do you know how hot that is? If there's anything women in the middle of life don't want, it's more heat. We are a smokeshow as-is. So thank you, but a marriage can effectively conduct its business with smoldering embers. That is enough.*

I know. I have a lot of thoughts. And this is just at the check-out, y'all. So if you see me and I look exhausted, it's because my brain is way more extroverted than I am and feels the need to speak up a lot.

Anyway. The magazines intrigue me. And if there is any magazine topic that's of particular interest to me, it is the capsule wardrobe—hands-down, no-questions-asked, back-up-every-other-topic-so-the-winner-can-come-forward-and-claim-her-prize. If magazines are any indication, women everywhere are clamoring for a capsule wardrobe, researching furiously so that they can get that particular part of their lives worked out and HANDLED.

Which begs the question: what in sam hill is a capsule wardrobe? I am so delighted to tell you.

A capsule wardrobe is a certain number of clothing items—maybe ten, maybe twelve, maybe even just seven—that you can mix and match, adding and subtracting accessories, to create seemingly infinite combinations. Take a couple of skirts, couple of pairs of pants, a few shirts, a jacket, a jumpsuit, a sweater, some timeless accessories—and boom! You have instantly simplified your life. You can now pack for any trip in less than forty-five seconds, and you can wear everything in your closet until you're eighty-seven without ever wearing the same combination.

Or something like that.

In theory I think a capsule wardrobe is an interesting idea; I hate standing in my closet and feeling like I have nothing to wear even though there are lots of clothes in front of me, so it seems like a collection of fewer, smarter options is a good idea. My problem, however, is that if you look at the pictures in most articles about capsule wardrobes, you quickly realize that no one you have never known dresses like this in real life.

Seriously. Not even in, like, 1956. And I feel like everybody was pretty dressed up back then.

Here's what I am going to tell you: I am a forty-nine-year-old working mama who spends a great deal of my free time either at live sporting events or on my couch, where I watch televised sporting events or an entire season of a TV series in one sitting. I sometimes even go walk on the treadmill.

So the fancy capsule wardrobes? No comprendo. Does not compute. Do not relate. I mean, I am never, under any circumstances, going to grab an expensive scarf, wrap it around my mid-section, and pretend like it's a skirt. Said scarf is also not going to serve as a swimsuit cover-up even one day during the precious time I have on this earth, primarily because I am too nice to do that to other people.

I am also not going to wake up on a Saturday morning and actually get dressed to go anywhere. I am going to put on workout clothes and do my very best to actually work out. I am not interested in some cutesy "weekend casual" shirt and slacks. There is no short-sleeved blouse in a geometric print with a dingdang bow at the neck that is ever going to be welcomed into my Saturday. Also, I have not worn a belt since 1998. It is the weekend. And GET AWAY FROM ME WITH YOUR BUTTONS.

Now I realize we've been talking about standing a lot in this book so far—standing through the grief, through the struggles, through the things God calls you to keep doing—but today, as a service to those of us who are forty and older (and maybe as some wisdom for those of you who are younger), I thought I would share my Real-Life Capsule Wardrobe with you for the days you can't stand for anything else because of all the time you spend standing in front of your stupid closet not knowing what to do. You might not be able to mix and match these pieces as efficiently as what you see in magazines, but if you're looking for comfort, you've come to the right place.

Here. I will even give my list a title.

Everybody Relax! 13 Essential Clothing Items for Middle Age

Here we go.

1. Oversized T-shirts

Look. They're not glamorous, but have mercy they're practical. And I'm not saying you should wear ones that look like sacks unless that's your personal preference; however, a T-shirt that's long enough to wear with workout leggings, to throw on before you take your kids through carpool, and—STAND BACK—to serve as a low-maintenance swimsuit cover-up—well, it is a gift that keeps on giving.

I love a college T-shirt, a sporting event T-shirt, a Free People T-shirt, or a vacation destination T-shirt, but please do walk in the freedom of your personal preferences. I understand that some people resist oversized T-shirts because they don't want people to think they've gained weight or they feel like big T-shirts make them look larger than they actually are. That's why I am going to share some news that will set you free: you do not have to care about that. Absolutely, be healthy. For sure. But also: BE COMFORTABLE. Enjoy some oversized cotton! It is your friend!

2. Good jeans (white, blue, black, gray—pick your poison)

It took me a long time to learn this lesson, but I'm grateful I finally did: good jeans are an investment. That means I don't buy them very often. I've owned my very favorite pair of jeans for four years, and they have served me well. They go with pretty much everything, they don't bag out in the waist or the knees, and they do some favors for my legs and, um, "hindquarters" (that's the term Mama liked to use). Yes, I am well aware that no one is looking at my legs or hindquarters, but I still enjoy feeling good in my nicer clothes (and in the case of jeans, my Sunday clothes—because I wear jeans to church almost every week).

Also, as a matter of personal conviction, I am doing my best to stand firm against the ripped jean trend because I have no desire to buy clothes that are already torn up. I feel like this is responsible adult behavior.

3. At-home bra

Anybody who has visited one of America's theme parks knows that we are smack-dab in the middle of an undergarment crisis in this country. We're not doing a great job of discerning our undergarment needs, particularly when it comes to bras. Maybe we want to be a 36 when we're actually a 42. Maybe we think we're a C cup when we're actually a DD. Maybe we think a lined camisole can take care of our needs, but NOT SO FAST, because that camisole just revealed way more about you I personally have a right to know.

Now, I realize that no one asked, but here are my personal guidelines in these challenging undergarment times: when I'm in public, I'm going to wear a bra in my actual size. Not the size I wish I was or the size I was in 2001. Things change and shift as we age. I try to support those things accordingly, as I would like to reach my sixties and not have to move those things out of the way when I fasten my jeans.

I trust that all of my vague vaguery has been crystal clear.

Where undergarments get trickier, however, is in the privacy of our own homes. On one hand, MY HOUSE, MY RULES, IT WAS FOR FREEDOM I WAS MADE FREE. On the other hand, we have company sometimes, or family comes to town, not to mention that I have a teenage son who has friends, and I would prefer not to traumatize anyone while I'm scrambling eggs for the group. That's why a good at-home bra is so valuable. I prefer something really soft, something with support, and something that can even transition to the gym if need be. My current favorite is something called the Funday bra, and while I think that is technically an oxymoron, it gets the job done. It's not quite as restrictive as a sports bra, and I daresay it's comfortable.

Make no mistake, though. As soon as everybody goes home, that sucker's coming off. This is my inalienable right as an American.

4. Workout leggings (yoga pants are also acceptable)

There are so many reasons I love workout leggings. For one thing, they're great for working out. They're lightweight, they're incredibly comfortable, and Lycra makes my legs happy. They're my go-to on weekends, my favorite for the gym, and my secret weapon for feeling strong (I have no idea why; but they sort of make me want to kick things). I feel like I've tried a good chunk of major brands, so I've learned some leggings lessons the hard way. If they're too thin or the fabric isn't great, they can be see-through (more power to you if that's how you roll, but I enjoy some coverage), and some brands seem like they're cut for junior sizes and not for someone who, as my friend Kasey would say, has a grown woman's bootie. Also, some brands don't breathe well, which is a nice way of saying that they are BURNING UP HOT, SOMEONE PLEASE RESCUE ME FROM THIS STRETCHY PANT PERIL.

So. Be wise when you select your workout leggings, but enjoy, my friends. What a fine companion they are. And in case you're wondering, my faves? The (discontinued) Lucy Perfect Core leggings (a modern wonder), and Brooks Greenlight Capris—the absolute perfect blend of lightweight and supportive.

5. Shorts

Hey. I get it. You're not sixteen anymore (or maybe you are, in which case let me follow the lead of Ms. Ramona Singer from *The Real Housewives of New York* to say *kadooz to you*), and you feel sort of self-conscious about your legs because they're vein-y in places and you're not a huge fan of your knees.

Here's what I have to say about that: It gets hot. Wear your shorts. You look great.

Also: If everybody's legs looked like Carrie Underwood's, then Carrie's legs wouldn't get the reverence and honor they're due. Her legs need for our legs to look like regular legs so that her legs can continue to be the standard-bearer.

So see? Wearing your shorts is actually an act of service to Carrie Underwood's legs. This is sort of like a ministry.

Wear your shorts.

You look great.

6. That dress you bought at TJ Maxx

When I was younger I used to think about what my life would be like as an adult, and I always imagined that I would need a lot of dresses. After all, I would likely be going to all manner of Fancy Places to attend a variety of Fancy Functions, and it would only be right and appropriate to have an assortment—a variety, if you will—of dresses on hand for all of the Very Special Occasions.

Here's how many Fancy Functions I attended last year: One. Uno.

Here's how many Fancy Functions I've attended so far this year: Zero plus zero equals zero.

My point is that if you're going somewhere that requires wearing a dress, just go ahead and dig out the one you bought at TJ Maxx that time you and your sister-in-law went shopping after the day after Christmas and you spotted the dress on the clearance rack and decided it would be fun to wear something sparkly on New Year's Eve, only when New Year's Eve rolled around it sounded like a lot of effort so you stayed home and made queso and watched Ryan Seacrest for twenty minutes before you climbed in bed at 10:00 p.m.

That dress. Wear that one. It'll be fantastic.

7. Wedges/Booties

I don't care what you're wearing; it'll look cuter if you pair it with wedges or booties.

Wait. Hold on: two exceptions: workout shorts and workout leggings.

Everything else? Gold.

8. Quality pajama bottoms

First, let me explain what I mean by "quality." This has nothing to do with cost and everything to do with durability. Good pajama bottoms will get softer as you wear them, but that does not mean they should become fragile. They shouldn't shrink—another issue with inferior brands—and what was meant to be full-length shouldn't become capri.

Second, beware of cute pajama bottoms masquerading as quality ones. Personally I've seen many a pair of adorable plaids or fun prints, and I daresay I've been hopeful as I've walked toward them in the store. However, if the fabric is stiff, you need to walk away. Stiff fabric won't breathe—I don't care if you give it an oxygen tank and a mask.

I would also add that fleece pajama bottoms are darlin' on your Christmas card. They're garbage when it comes to getting a sound night's sleep. Unless you find spontaneous combustion restful, of course.

Third, do not forsake the GAP of your youth. GAP is consistently the very best for all things comfy, affordable, and durable in the way of pajama bottoms. A couple of years ago their sleep leggings became one of my most trusted companions. What a blessing.

9. Comfortable running shoes/sneakers

Fine. Whatever. Maybe this is super obvious and you just rolled your eyes because really? This is one of the things I feel like I need to spell out in detail?

Yes. Yes, I do.

Here's why.

Last summer David and I went to New York City on an anniversary trip, and because I wanted to look cute on the plane (don't @ me) (I was going away with my husband) (have to tend to those smoldering embers, you know), I wore some slip-on sandals with a three-inch heel. When we dropped off our luggage at the hotel, David asked if I wanted to change shoes, and I said, "Oh, no. I'm so fine. These are really comfortable." I could tell he was skeptical, but he went along with my plan.

An hour later, we were probably twenty blocks south of our hotel, and I was *this close* to throwing those sandals in the trash. Being barefoot on the streets of New York City seemed preferable to enduring the torment of shuffling along in those backless thongs from Sheol that had rubbed my feet raw.

I had a similar experience in a pair of Birkenstocks at Universal Studios in Orlando. I would go into detail, but the trauma is still too great.

Which brings me to my point: I love a great pair of shoes. I believe I've made that clear. But when it comes to walking long distances, traversing an amusement park, or running around the city that never sleeps, my arches and my ankles appreciate the support of a well-made athletic shoe.

Plus, sneakers and running shoes are CUTE these days! They go with everything, so you can substitute them for sandals or flats or heels. You'll be crazy stylish, and your feet will be so grateful.

This is starting to feel like an infomercial. My apologies. Just get a good pair of comfortable sneakers and walk to your heart's content.

10. Shirts that cover your behind

Of everything I've mentioned, this one just might be my personal key to selecting clothes during the work week without stressing out. I walk in my closet, and I select my pants for the day. We can't wear blue jeans to work, but we can wear denim. This means I typically pick out white jeans, gray jeans, or black jeans—maybe corduroys if I'm feeling like a woman on the edge. I slip on either wedges or booties—depending on the season—and then I select a shirt that covers my behind.

This is a key to my personal peace and happiness. You may enjoy a shorter top, but for me, a shirt that's longer in the back is one of life's great comforts. You don't have to worry about what your pants are doing. You don't have to worry about wearing some sort of specialty underwear that features a control top but really just makes you feel like a can of biscuits that is begging the back of a spoon to set it free.

For me, it simplifies the process of getting ready. I pick my clothes, and after that, it's just necklace/earrings/wedding rings/watch.

So to review: denim, shoes, STCYB™, accessories.

Look how easy that was!

11. Kimonos

To be clear, I'm not referring to a traditional Japanese garment when I say "kimono." I'm referring to an American trend that's become popular in recent years. It's a light, oftentimes patterned jacket—usually made from a thin polyester or satin—that's worn as a top layer. The great thing about a kimono is that it's an instant outfit maker. Pick out a pair of jeans, a plain T-shirt of any color, then throw on your kimono (with either wedges or booties, of course). All of a sudden—voilà—YOU LOOK FANTASTIC. Look how pulled together you are! This is the way to tackle clothing dilemmas for date night, girls' night, or a night out with friends. Basically it's Garanimals for Grown Women, and to that I say IT'S ABOUT TIME.

12. Old sweatshirt

Oh, I understand that kids today love their hoodies and their fleeces and their Woolies. Good for them. All of those options seem perfectly serviceable.

But back in the day, we wore sweatshirts. There was nothing "fitted" about them. They were big, and they were warm, and they were essentially fabric boxes with a neck cut out. To this very day you can walk in my closet and find a Mississippi State sweatshirt that I have owned for at least twenty-five years, and I will never part with it. It's nothing special, I know—there are certainly more attractive options if you're on the hunt for comfort and warmth—but every once in a while I like to hang out with the twenty-three-year-old who still lives inside my head, and that sweatshirt helps me remember her. Nobody has to know.

13. Black pants

From time to time you need somewhat nicer pants that you don't hate that aren't jeans.

These will be fine.

So there you have it. Real clothes for real women living their real lives.

Be on the look-out for my follow-up article: *Five Tower Fans That Will Keep Your Closet Cool!*

CHAPTER 8

It's So Nice to Finally Meet You

Let me set the scene.

It was Christmas Eve. Alex was six. And for the first time in our married lives, we didn't have any extended family in town for Christmas. Because of the way everyone's travel plans had worked out, Mama and Daddy wouldn't be at our house until Christmas afternoon, and Sister and Barry wouldn't arrive until a couple of days after Christmas. Throughout the previous week I had been telling myself that it was *fine, really, it would all be so fine*, but the reality was that I had a terrible case of the sads. It had been a brutally difficult year—so much job- and money-related stress—not to mention that I had turned forty despite the fact that I still fancied myself twenty-three in my head.

No joke. That fortieth birthday hit me like a runaway train. And truth be told, I was pretty content to just lay down where it left me. Preferably with a soft blanket and a backlog of *Veronica Mars* episodes.

So about mid-afternoon on our lonely Christmas Eve, David and I decided that it was going to be oh-so-sad if the three of us just sat at home all day. We came up with the idea of going to look at Christmas lights after it was dark and then stopping somewhere for a quick supper. It was an option highly preferable to spending Christmas Eve with the aforementioned blanket and back-to-back episodes of crime fighting with Kristen Bell—delightful and witty though she is.

Alex was overjoyed to climb in his backseat booster seat when we left the house, and as was the norm when he was six, he brought his beloved Froggy (a stuffed frog) and Monkey (a stuffed monkey) (who says we're not creative namers) along for the ride. His enthusiasm was contagious as he "oooh"'d and "ahhh"'d at Christmas lights, and by the time we were ready for supper, my formerly Grinch-y mood was on the upswing. *WE ARE MAKING MEMORIES,* I thought. *SUCH A PRECIOUS TIME! THE WONDER OF CHRISTMAS THROUGH THE EYES OF A CHILD!*

Waves of optimism and hope washed over me for upwards of fifteen minutes. And then, as we started to look for somewhere to eat supper, we realized that Popeye's was our only option.

Now please don't misunderstand. I adore Popeye's. I even joke sometimes that I minored in Popeye's at Mississippi State. I love their spicy fried chicken, I love their French fries, and I even love their red beans and rice despite the fact that it is woefully deficient in red beans. Mostly it's just a brown sauce and rice, but I am certainly not complaining about any aspect of the Cajun-flavored goodness. It is evidence of the Lord's common grace, amen.

However, on Christmas Eve in the year of our Lord 2009, we rolled up to the Popeye's about twenty-five minutes before closing. There were no other customers, and seconds after we placed our orders, we turned and realized that most of the employees appeared to be having a Christmas party in a far corner of the dining area. It didn't take long for our food to be ready, and as the three of us sat around the

table, David and I doing our best to be merry while half-heartedly digging into our Christmas Eve chicken, I made up my mind that I was
presently and fully experiencing the worst Christmas Eve of my life.

Seriously. If you wrote a children's book about it, you could call
it something really catchy like *Santa's Last Drumstick.* Or better yet,
Santa, Why Is Mama Sad?

We were just about to gather up our trash when one of the employees stopped by our table and offered Alex a sugar-covered Christmas
cookie. It was such a kind gesture—and so appreciated by the six-
year-old at the table—but, as David and I later discussed, it was also a
disconcerting moment of clarity:

> *Just a hunch, but we might be lacking in the "community"*
> *department.*

JUST. A. HUNCH.

Perhaps I can provide some back story.

By and large—and I think this is an accurate self-assessment—
after Alex was born I adjusted pretty well to motherhood. I mean, I
was tired, and I couldn't keep up with the laundry, and I struggled
with balancing work and motherhood, but in terms of *Whoa, there's
another person in our family now,* I think I did okay. I fed him, watered
him, hugged him, read to him, and, as you do, gradually got the hand
of integrating a new little life into our everyday routine. In fact, David
and I quickly realized that living with Alex Hudson might well be the
most fun either of us had ever had, so day by day, we just made it work.
It seems to me that's what most people do.

Where I struggled, however—and where I really let fear grab hold—was making friends with other mamas and other families. This was a totally unexpected development. I made friends easily during the other formative stages of my life—high school, college, career, early married days—but for some reason the motherhood / family friendships confounded and intimidated me. Fortunately I had a couple of friends from work and church who transitioned into mama life about the same time that I did, and those relationships continued to be fun and easy. I also had a Bible study group of wonderful women who were in a different stage of life than I was. But as far as befriending a new face at Mother's Day Out or the playground or Chick-fil-A? Or making small talk at the Thanksgiving program? That was a nope-ity / no ma'am / nope for me. I never said it out loud, of course, but my general attitude from 2003–2008 was *I'll just sit over here and check Facebook on my Blackberry if it's all the same to y'all.*

Looking back I've really tried to figure out why it wasn't easy to build new relationships with people in the same stage of life, and my best, most honest explanation—and I've thought about this a lot over the last two or three years—is that I both expected and feared judgment. I went back to work the fall after Alex was born, and since just about everyone I knew was a stay-at-home mama, I convinced myself that putting myself out there with new "mom" friendships meant that I would inevitably face disapproval about my work-away-from-home status. Clearly these were my own issues—nothing any friend or potential friend had verbalized to me—but my insecurity about being a working mama bossed me around more than I liked to admit.

Basically the narrative I created for myself was this: all the other mamas I saw during the course of a day were doing Mommy & Me classes at the gym while I was toiling in the salt mines of high school

English classes and trying to get 10th graders to understand the themes of *Julius Caesar*.

We would have nothing in common.

I wish I could rewind time and give myself a good talkin'-to about this line of thinking. It was so unfair to everybody: to other mamas, to other families, to myself, and to women in general. I took what should have been a time of great camaraderie and reduced it to categories. For the record, that was really short-sighted and dumb.

And then, when Alex was two, I started a blog, and whatever I was lacking in relational connection with other women here in Birmingham I started to find online. Even typing that makes me cringe a little bit, but it's the straight-up truth. And a few months into blogging, when I connected with my dear friend Melanie—who also worked outside the home, who also had one child, who also loved to write funny stuff, who also followed college football with a fervor that some might consider troubling—there was an almost instant ease to our friendship. Keep in mind that this was around 2006, so the odds of me telling my coworkers or family members that I made a new friend on the internet were initially slim to THAT CAN JUST BE MY LITTLE SECRET, but over the course of a year or so, Melanie became such a big part of my life that she might as well have lived in the same ZIP code. I felt safe with her, understood by her, and incredibly grateful to have a friend who totally related to the blogging and writing part of my life. There's not a doubt in my mind that the Lord intended for us to walk our writing road together, and our friendship continues to be one of the greatest, most unexpected gifts of my adult life.

By the time my little family made our fateful trip to the Popeye's on Christmas Eve, Melanie and I had been close for several years, and one day when I was apparently awash in vulnerability, I confessed to Melanie that I was teetering on the edge of lonely. Work and writing demanded so much of my time and energy, so I didn't get to invest in my friendships with other mamas like I had hoped, not to mention that David and I really needed some couple friends. Yes, I had Bible study mentors who were great sources of comfort and wisdom, but I realized I was missing the consistent companionship of people who were my age-ish. So was David.

And that, my friends, is, at least in part, how you end up at an almost-closed Popeye's for Christmas Eve supper. No doubt that fateful trip to Popeye's provided some hard, incontrovertible evidence about a couple of areas of my life:

1. Sad or not sad, I'm pretty much always game for a spicy two-piece meal with red beans and rice.
2. David and I needed to do more to plug into real-live life here in Birmingham, to build stronger relationships and community in the place we call home.

And it might be wise to do that, like, ASAP.

Lest we celebrate Easter at a close-to-closing Captain D's.

The next few years were full of so many baby steps.

One of the main baby steps was some honest self-examination, especially on the couple friends front. I mean, if you've by and large struggled to connect with other couples despite the fact that you've been a member of the same local church for upwards of ten years, it's a good idea to dig down in the "why" of that so you can deal with it and hopefully not repeat the pattern. It ended up taking a long time to get to the core of it, which means there were periods of deep introspection alternated with some hefty doses of can't-be-bothered-to-think-about-this-anymore. Eventually, though, I started to understand our three biggest obstacles to committing to real, up-close community right here in Birmingham.

1. **Shame that caused me to fear judgment**

If you've lived in the land of the American evangelical church for long enough, you may have grown accustomed to hearing couple-stories that sound like a variation on a theme: *we met in college, we were leaders in college ministry, we were discipled by the most incredible, godly people who were about ten years older, we fell in love, we couldn't wait to serve the Lord together for the rest of our lives, and now we only want to make His name known.*

The couple is holding *both* hands while they say this, of course.

And I'm exaggerating, clearly. Plus, people with those stories actually aren't "those couples" because they have all sorts of issues too. But I had a *perception* that we were surrounded in our church and our community by a whole lot of "perfect couples," and we just wouldn't measure up.

Don't misunderstand. We weren't running a crime ring out of our basement or anything like that (and if we had been, Jesus would have met us right there). But David and I didn't have a story that was nearly so neat and tidy. We had both worked hard to push Jesus away in our twenties, we didn't adjust to marriage easily, and whatever sitcom-ish notions we had of wedded bliss blew up in our faces during those first few years of marriage.

Basically I wanted to be one of those couples with a nicer, neater story. I even kind of wanted to hold both hands (though I am in general not a fan of holding any hands at all). And over time I had made up my mind that if we went into a small group or couple's Bible study, we'd be judged and found unworthy of belonging.

So, you know, that was a road block.

2. **Good, old-fashioned laziness**

We really liked being at home. We really liked watching television. I really liked to put on my pajamas after church and then write for the rest of the afternoon. We both had obligations that took us away from the house on weeknights, so when we'd talk about doing some kind of discipleship activity as a couple, we'd always come back to the fact that we didn't want more commitments; we wanted less. Community would likely require more of us than we were willing to give. And—if I can just say it one more time—WE ENJOYED US SOME TV, AMEN.

3. **Skepticism**

We'd never find people we could trust, right? And even if we did, it wouldn't last, right? And by the way, we would for sure be (secretly) judged, right? I'm convinced that skepticism is what keeps 90% of us away from a deep dive into a local church community. Maybe we think a church's theology needs to be beefier and we don't want to put our trust in a pastor who doesn't have seventeen degrees from assorted seminaries and Bible colleges. Maybe we fear getting tangled up in a church with a large number of people whose primary hobby is "discernment ministry" on the internet. Maybe we've had a bad church experience in the past, and we can't help but wonder if Jesus is just the bait to lure us into giving the church lots of money. Maybe we think a church is going to pressure us to vote a certain way or champion certain causes. There are all sorts of issues that convince us to keep church community at arm's length, and it takes time, prayer, faith, and trust to begin to bridge that divide.

I know that for some people this stuff is effortless. But for David and me, not so much—mainly because getting healthier relationally meant we had to address struggles on multiple levels. I only knew a few of the moms in Alex's grade (and BLESS THE LORD for those sweet women), so I didn't have much "mama community" in my life. David and I didn't have many overlapping relationships, so we weren't really digging deep with other couples. And since David and I weren't in a small group together at church, we didn't participate in the support, accountability, and encouragement that small groups can provide for marriages.

We eventually came to realize that our commitments and distractions made it easy to pretend that the issue of real-life community wasn't quite as pressing as it felt on that fateful Popeye's Christmas Eve. We'd feel our collective disconnect and just push it away. David eventually switched jobs and was happily swamped at work, so on the weekends he was perfectly content to just hang out with Alex and me. By the time we headed into the back half of Alex's elementary school years, I had convinced myself that my working life would likely continue to interfere with my relational life. It seemed like that was just how it was going to be for us, like maybe we weren't meant for all that "deep community" stuff after all.

Except.

When Alex was in 5th grade, he started playing football. It was his first team sport after giving up on soccer a couple of years before.

I didn't necessarily expect for football to take—David and I had no idea if he would like it—but we felt like it was important for him to try something new and plug into a team dynamic.

As it turned out, he loved football. He wasn't a superstar athlete, but he loved his team, he loved his coaches, and he even loved the practices. Football, much to our surprise, was a fit.

And football forced me to realize something about the other families on the team: they knew each other. They knew each other's kids. The familiarity between those families was strangely comforting and inspiring to me. And as I watched and listened to the other mamas when I dropped off or picked up from practice, I realized that they were the most delightful women—the most delightful families—and our ever-deepening comfort with staying just a wee bit isolated was going to make us miss out on knowing them.

Over the course of that first football season, here's what I discovered: I wasn't okay with missing them.

So here's what that meant: ready or not, it was officially time for a change.

———————

I want to be so clear about something just in case I haven't been. I have had wonderful friends at every point in my married life, and I am so grateful for the people who stayed in it with me when I was content with relational distance. The bait of isolation was not only tasty, it was filling, and when Alex was younger, it felt more comfortable to stay closed off from other families. As Alex got older, however, David and I realized that we wanted and needed to do better about opening ourselves up to the relational opportunities that presented themselves in our day-to-day life, and on a spiritual level we wanted to do local church life in a deeper, more meaningful way.

This means that we started doing the stuff that, you know, HUMAN BEINGS do. We talked to people at football games. My friend and coworker, Heather, has long known everybody in five counties, so when she would introduce me to moms from Alex's grade (of course she knew most of them before I did, because she is intentional and also neighborly), I sincerely wanted to get to know them.

This all sounds ridiculous, I realize. But I am not kidding when I tell you that it felt like mostly starting from scratch. It felt like being the new kid in school—only I had been a part of Alex's school since he was in K4.

And during that 5th grade year—specifically during that 5th grade football season—something changed. We started to know the people sitting in the stands with us. I figured out what kids went with what parents. Again, I know this sounds ridiculous, but teaching English during Alex's elementary school years meant that I hadn't plugged into mom activities during the school day at all. And as those faces in the bleachers became more familiar, I started recognizing them in the grocery store, at Starbucks, and even in church. I realized that a lot of those moms had older children who were at the high school with me, and we'd visit in the parking lot or in the front office when they stopped by school.

It's the strangest thing. When I finally started looking for people, I actually started to see them.

So that spring, when Alex's 5th grade class gave his teacher a baby shower, I not only stopped by to drop off a gift—I stayed. I plopped down on a window seat and I visited with Amelia's mom and Mae's mom and I didn't even sweat to death. And at the end of the school year, I went to Field Day—which I had never, ever done. I even took snacks and served them and visited with the other moms while the kids competed. I KNEW PEOPLE'S NAMES, y'all.

The Lord is faithful and worthy to be praised.

Even as I'm writing this, I'm thinking, *Oh my gosh. This all sounds so dumb.* But when you've made a habit out of feeling mostly disconnected, the process of getting to know people without facing scorn or scoffing or shame feels just a little bit like a miracle. When you've made one excuse after another for why you don't have time to get to know other moms or families, the realization that you don't have to play that part forever is a combination of relief and unexpected grace, with a tiny little bit of grief mixed in.

Because you missed some things, you know?

By the beginning of Alex's 6th grade year, the motherhood part of my life felt exponentially healthier. In fact, the Friday night before school started, we took Alex to Student Ministry kick-off at our church, and we realized that there were four or five other kids from our church in his class. Our families stood around, excitedly chatting about what a fun year it would be and what a phenomenal teacher they were going to have, and my new-ish friend Kasey looked at me and said, "You know, we should start a small group with some of our school families."

"Here? At church?" I asked.

"Yep," she answered. "We totally should. Y'all pray about that."

I told David about it after we got home, and unlike the other 402 times we had considered joining a small group together, he said, "Hmmmm. I might be interested in that."

So we prayed about it. So did Kasey and her husband, Joel. So did my new-ish friend Stephanie and her husband, Joey. So did a couple of other families that Kasey and Joel knew from college and music ministry.

And on the second Sunday in January—at the beginning of the 2nd semester of Alex's 6th grade year—David and I began our Sunday morning at church with our new—wait for it!—*small group friends*.

Look at the Lord, y'all.

It took a little over six years after our memorable Christmas Eve at Popeye's, but by diggity David and I finally found our way to consistent community in our church. I was and am so grateful to have formed relationships with other moms in Alex's grade, and then for a part of that to carry over into our church life—well, it's been something really special.

You can have it, too, you know. Whether you're single or divorced or a college student or a newlywed or a person in a relationship with someone who wants nothing to do with the church. You can choose to live in community with your church family.

Because listen. I have a tendency sometimes to get eye-roll-y about our preoccupation with personal transformation in the evangelical church, but I cannot overstate this: our small group community has completely changed not just our Sunday mornings, but the day-to-day dynamics of our family. It has been the biggest blast to dig deep into faith and marriage and parenting with other people. It has been such a comfort to struggle together. Sure, I've known for a long time that Scripture prioritizes living in community. Turns out that's because it's a pretty awesome practice for the life of believers and the health of the church.

Fancy that.

⎯⎯●⎯⎯⎯

This past Sunday we went to lunch after church.

There were nine of us: Stephanie, Joey, and their Ella; Kasey, no Joel (he was on call)—but with their Ashby and Sam; then David, me, and our Alex. At this point our lunch outings seem pretty routine, but I distinctly remember the first Sunday we all went to Chuy's after small group and church. I remember wondering if our small group experiment would stick.

Spoiler alert: it has stuck. We've been in it to win it for over three years now.

And this past Sunday at Metro Diner—well, it was pretty typical. The adults broke down the events of the week while the kids sat at the end of the table and laughed about stuff on their phones. The three teenagers talked about an upcoming dance at school, and then one of the three (okay, it was mine) overstepped some boundaries when he tried to put in his two cents about one of the girl's opinions. At that point Kasey and I swapped seats so I could hunker down next to my beloved offspring and lovingly instruct him to SIMMER DOWN WITH THE SARCASM. This is the case almost every single time— one of the kids gets a little too comfortable / opinionated / full of sass and fire and finds him or herself the object of some spirited parental fellowship—so right then and there, as best we can, we break it down and talk it through and make it right. And no matter what's going on in the way of correction, the adults keep on keepin' on with conversation that ranges from the silly to the serious to the spiritual.

Over the last three years our small group has dealt with broken relationships and broken dreams and more than our fair share of broken bones. We've analyzed the latest documentary we've all watched and loved, we've spoken hard truths, and over and over again, when conversations have strayed too far in the direction of gossip, someone (I'll be honest—it's usually Kasey) has piped up and said, "You know what? This is not necessary. This is not helpful."

More than anything else, I think, we have refused to pretend or pose or play games with one another. That practice alone has been life changing.

And last week, after Alex and I had gotten to the bottom of some things at the Metro Diner, after he and the girls had put their relational pieces back together, after I had taken a break from the group and walked outside and tried to calm down because a teenage boy's many opinions can sometimes fire me all the way up, after we had said our good-byes and walked to our cars and headed in the direction of home, I leaned back against the passenger seat headrest and remembered something I forget all too easily.

When Alex was a toddler and I started to suspect that he might be an only child—something that initially wasn't on my maternal radar—I prayed more times than I could count that the Lord would give him friends that feel like family.

And last Sunday, even though I was sort of ticked off and wasn't great company for the last twenty minutes of our lunch, I sat in some fresh awareness and gratitude that the Lord has flat-out done it in terms of friends feeling like family. He's done it for David and me too—even though we didn't always know to pray that for ourselves.

So yes. We are heard and safe and seen in our small group community. We love each other a lot. Our deep desire is to spur on one another to "proclaim the Lord's greatness" and "exalt his name together" (Ps. 34:3). And maybe my favorite thing is that while the people in our small group are some of our very best friends, they aren't our only friends. For some reason I thought committing to community would create a "lock down" effect where we'd focus only on a certain group of people, but my experience has been the opposite. Community has opened us up, not shut us down. We have a home base now—that much is for sure—and knowing where home base is has made us feel a whole lot more free to move into new relational territory. In fact, the last few years of developing friendships with the moms in Alex's grade—well, I just wouldn't take anything for being able to know and love them. They have taught me so much about building community with each other and with our kids. Obviously I still treasure my friends from college and writing and work—I cannot imagine life without them—and I hope I bring a better me to those friendships now that David and I are more planted and rooted in our lives here in Birmingham.

It's weird. So much of these last several years has been about learning to stand: stand up for myself, stand for what's right, stand in the face of adversity. But listen. There's also something to be said for committing to the practice of sitting down in the company of believers, sitting down face-to-face with funny, wise people who love the Lord and love His church, sitting down with men and women (and teenagers!) who will tell you the truth, love you unconditionally, and, like Aaron and Hur, lift your arms when necessary (stay tuned, by the way—we'll talk more about those guys later). I would even argue that what happens when we're sitting strengthens us for the standing.

Deep, genuine fellowship in the context of the local church absolutely makes the good times better and the bad times bearable. It absolutely makes the battles easier. It absolutely makes the grace and mercy of God more tangible and real.

The only disappointment?

We haven't all been to Popeye's together.

I trust the Lord will redeem that in His time.

CHAPTER 9

Putting My Foot Down

One of the nicest things about this particular stage of life is that, for the most part, I've lost the will to pretend to care about stuff that I really don't give two cents about, and I'll have no part in any charade where I'm required to feign interest. You might feel like this behavior borders on rude, but it's not. It's just honest. This means that you might not walk away from a conversation with me about, say, cold-shouldered tops feeling validated regarding your affection for them, but you will walk away knowing where I stand. And for the record, I stand on the opposite end of the universe from cold-shouldered shirts, as I have no patience for a sleeve that refuses to commit.

Make up your mind, cold-shoulder tops.

Be sleeveless or be a full-on sleeve. You can't have it all the ways, cold-shoulder. Pick a lane.

In my younger days I would have gone along with the cold-shoulder enthusiasm, and even if I didn't love that particular style, I would have acted like I did because I wouldn't have wanted to hurt your feelings—and I might have even worried that you'd be angry with me for seeing the cold-shoulder situation differently than you. I believe we covered some of these issues in a previous chapter.

Now, however, here's what I know: if you're going to get your feelings hurt over my views on a cold-shouldered top, you may be operating at a level of sensitivity / borderline co-dependency that I'm just not going to enable. AND if you're going to get angry with me because I don't like your shirt, then I have a hunch that we're probably not going to go the distance with our friendship, so it's better if we both go ahead and adjust our relational expectations accordingly.

This is middle age, everyone. Welcome to my no-nonsense party.

There are several factors that I believe have empowered the side of my personality that's a little more straight-shooting. One is the sanctifying work of Jesus, who *never not even one time* jumped on somebody's inconsequential bandwagon for fear that He might offend them if He didn't. Two is that I've finally learned people can openly disagree without the world coming to a fiery end. And three—just to be totally candid—is that I'm a good bit more feisty these days because I'm perimenopausal and I'm hot all the time and SOMEBODY GET THAT A/C CRANKED DOWN BEFORE I SWEAT TO DEATH.

So yes. It's a combination of things.

Anyway.

I promise that I don't walk around in a perpetual state of outrage—far from it, in fact—but every so often, I'll run across something that pushes my buttons, then stands on my buttons, then hops up and down on my buttons until I scream at it to leave me alone.

If you ask me, it's high time we stand against those things and hold them accountable.

LET JUSTICE BE SERVED.

I'll start.

- *Highlighting/contouring with makeup like we're walking cosmetics ads.* I love shopping for makeup. I love me some Sephora and some Blue Mercury and some quality skin care products. However, this trend where everybody is a make-up artist and hold on just a second and I'll show you how to take this palette with nine bronzers and sculpt cheekbones out of air? No ma'am. I'll feel a lot better about our friendship if I have a solid idea about what your actual face looks like. For example, that shadow you see above my cheekbone? That is a straight-up late-forties crevasse. I have no need to create the illusion of depth in this area of my face. Just look what nature did!

- *Arguing on social media.* Here's what we all need from social media right now: puppy videos, dance team routines (preferably including mascots), thirty-second cooking videos, surprise reunions between deployed service members and their families, and anything with Bruno Mars because Bruno Mars is the musical equivalent of a confetti cannon. What we don't need on social media right now is any more arguing. As many people have already pointed out, the number of times when someone has said, "You know I was really leaning one way on this issue, but then I read through someone's angry Twitter comments and changed my mind! I see that thing completely differently now!" is NO TIMES. It does not happen. Not this side of heaven, at least. And I'm pretty sure it won't happen in heaven either because there's no way the Lord lets us argue via social media in heaven. Assuming social media is even there, of course.

- *People who stand around and swing an imaginary golf club.* WE GET IT. YOU PLAY GOLF. PLEASE ACCEPT OUR CONGRATULATIONS.

- *Sports fans who fan harder than anyone has ever fanned.* A live sporting event—particularly at the high school or college level—is one of my top five favorite pastimes. I have often said that if I lived in Starkville, home of my beloved Mississippi State, I would show up for whatever games/matches were scheduled on any given day. Disc golf? Sure. Barrel racing? Save me a seat. Field hockey? Of course, but I may be running a few minutes late because I want to paint up before I get there. My point is that I love a live competition, but lately, no matter which sport I'm watching, I seem to find myself seated next to sports enthusiasts who take it to a level that's borderline unbearable—a level of enthusiasm and hype and player-familiarity so chock-full of try-hard that I want to find a corner and plug my ears and cover my entire person with a blanket until the flexing and the stomping and the unrelenting chorus of "THIS IS *YOUR* GAME, T-MAC MY DUDE!" mercifully subsides.

   T-Mac doesn't know you, friend.

   Sit down.

- *Hats as functionless accessories.* I'm not talking about wearing a hat for the purposes of warmth or camouflaging your unwashed hair or protecting your head/face from the sun. I'm not even talking about adding a fascinator when you're an acquaintance of the British royal family and expected to wear an interesting headpiece with your wedding attire. I'm not talking about dressing up for the Kentucky Derby or for a special church service. I'm talking about getting dressed for a regular ole day, getting your outfit and your hair and your (contoured!) make-up just like you like it, and then perching some sort of fedora on the back of your head just like it's necessary. This is some fresh foolishness. For one thing, that hat won't stay put for love nor money, so you've created a situation that requires the assistance of at least fourteen bobby pins poking into your skull. Second of all, if you're at a concert or the movies, you've created a visual impediment for the people behind you, especially since the brim of that hat is likely popped up at a ninety-degree angle. Third—and I hope you know that I say this in all Christian love and kindness—a hat worn for purely decorative purposes on an ordinary day feels like way too much effort. You are not a Christmas tree. You do not need a star on the top of your head in order to be completely accessorized. There's just no need to create a high-maintenance situation out of something that's meant to be practical and functional. You're welcome.

- *People who use their phones during movies.* I realize that we are a nation that fancies ourselves as exceptional multitaskers, so I understand how difficult it is for us to tear ourselves away from our 3x6 illuminated, handheld bosses. Our whole lives are on those things, and at any given moment we can read a text from Aunt Glenda, finish a spreadsheet from work, catch up on the president's latest Twitter firestorm (insert eye roll emoji here), or answer a seemingly urgent email from a potential new client. And while I get the temptation to be ever-available, ever-accessible, and ever-engaged, I just have to say: for the love of Pete, everybody, can we all agree to put away our phones for two hours in the movie theatre? Can we please watch *Black Panther* without Snapchatting people to let them know we're watching *Black Panther*? How many selfies do we actually need, anyway? Is our FOMO so out of hand that we can't possibly disconnect from the world for 120 minutes? I mean, I recognize that you've turned your brightness way down low so that the light from the phone won't disturb anyone (here's a hint: WE CAN ALL STILL SEE IT), but I would like to suggest that we just flip over el telefono so that it's case-side-up and make a pledge in our hearts to leave it be while we commit to the picture show. Thank you and have a blessed day.

- *People who grunt at the gym.* When I was a little girl and would do something that my mama deemed rude—like interrupt an adult or yell at someone across the church parking lot or sneeze a little too loudly at the dinner table—Mama would typically wait until we were someplace private to address the error of my ways. More often than not, she would conclude her challenge to do better with eight words: "Now Sophie, there's just no need for that." This is exactly how I feel when I'm at the gym with people who cannot lift five pounds of weight without grunting like they're trying to singlehandedly push Mount McKinley off of its base and then relocate it a mile down the road. Our gym has a policy that instructs us not to drop weights or make loud noises as we lift, and while most folks are courteous in that regard, there are several people who apparently left their copy of the rules inside their membership folders. There's one man (and I'm sure he's a perfectly lovely person in other aspects of his life) who grunts so loudly that, when I get to the gym and see his name on the sign-in sheet, I am tempted to leave. Spartacus made less noise when he fought the Romans. I'm not sure what this guy's history is, but I suspect there are some weightlifting sessions with the football team in his past, some bench-pressing sessions where everybody was trying to outlift and outgrunt one another. Unfortunately, he has transferred that (alleged) pattern of behavior to our small gym, and one day I'm afraid he will meet the collective wrath of 8–10 middle-aged women who will give him a good talkin'-to after we march across the gym floor in our Brooks running shoes and our yoga pants.

SIMMER DOWN, SIR. WE CAN HARDLY HEAR THE MUSIC OVER YOUR GRUNT-A-THON. YOU'RE LOUDER THAN A PASSEL OF PIGS. AND THERE'S JUST NO NEED FOR THAT.

So there you have it: the (critical) (clearly very serious) issues where I absolutely refuse to pretend. To be clear, it's not an exhaustive list, but I only have so much room in the chapter. And you know what? I imagine you could add a few items of your own. One of the things on your list might even be my name because you are super partial to your decorative hats. And that's okay. Pushing each other's buttons—accidentally or on purpose—is part of the human condition, isn't it?

Plus, it's all exacerbated by the fact that the Lord has given us SO. MANY. OPINIONS. And that's precisely where the Lord sets up camp and challenges me to do better every single day.

Because somewhere in the middle of all our opinions, we have to be willing to set aside our very strong preferences and our very deep desire to set all the bronzers on fire (I am speaking hypothetically, you understand) and choose to love one another more than we love our perceived rightness.

However, I would like to state for the record that I am totally right about there being no need for grunters at the gym.

And while I'm pretty sure that the Lord has asked me to stand on behalf of folks who prefer a phone-free environment at the movies, Scripture makes it clear that if I'm going to fight for anything, it needs to be for His people.

Even if their personal choices drive me all the way up the wall.

So how's that for some big picture perspective? I won't presume to speak for you, but I can say with some certainty that I need the reminder more often than I like to admit.

However, I'm really not backing down on the cold-shoulder shirts. Principles, you understand.

CHAPTER 10

When the World Keeps Screaming

This might surprise you, but lately I've noticed that the United States of America—land that I love—has gotten pretty extra with its crazy.

Or maybe I should say it like Mama would: y'all, we have lost our fool minds.

We duke it out with one another on our favorite social media platforms, and many times the ringleaders are people elected to serve us. We're tangled up about an endless array of topics—guns, immigration, trade, hate speech, racism, privilege, abortion, media, economic, and environmental issues—and for the most part, the referees have long left the building. We're hunkered down in our respective corners, screaming at the top of our lungs, clinging to our political parties just like they can save us. Based on the tone and tenor of our online discussions, you'd think that the kingdom to come will have an official logo that's an elephant or a donkey, not to mention an official news network. We yell and we rail and we blame and we name call. We answer questions by pointing fingers at the other side, and we defend absolutely indefensible behavior as long as said behavior benefits our side of the aisle.

I won't even get into how we condone and encourage behavior that we would never tolerate from our own children or employees or students or family members. Just suffice it to say that we're living in a bananapants level of chaos and dysfunction and discouragement and disaster.

It's been ramped up for the better part of four years.

And I'll shoot gut-level honest with you: I haven't been handling it well.

No matter how hard I try, no matter how hard I pray, I battle an overwhelming, nagging sense that the world is upside down. In addition to the hatefulness we direct at each other, our weather is erratic, natural disasters are frequent, mass shootings are rampant, and the leadership strategy at the federal level of government seems to rely heavily on setting things on fire and then either denying that there's smoke, screaming that it's all burning down, or trying to douse the flames with a water pistol.

It's beyond exhausting.

I talk about this stuff a lot with my friends because it weighs heavier on me than I would like, but I can't seem to shake it, and Lord knows I've tried. I've stopped listening to the news in my car. I've stopped watching the news in the evenings unless there's an election or some major national development. I try to read at least one newspaper a day because I am my daddy's child and feel some odd civic obligation to stay informed about what's going on in the world. Plus, I figure that reading the news gives me more time to process and hopefully makes me less reactionary about the day's events. I don't frequent message boards or partisan news sites. I don't chase down conspiracy theories.

You will never hear me use the phrases "crisis actor" or "deep state." I can smell propaganda masking as news from a mile away.

So as best I know how, I have established some current events boundaries.

But the state of the world, the divisiveness and hatefulness in the United States—combined with the fact that we're content to stand idly by while people in leadership stoke the aforementioned divisiveness and hatefulness, and we're apparently willing to let the fires burn as long as the economy is good—it's so heavy, y'all.

I know that God can hold it.

I know that.

And that's comforting. Because the weight of it feels like a lot—sometimes even like it's way more than we can collectively bear.

———

There are several topics that seem to run on an endless loop in my brain, topics I never tire of considering and pondering and discussing and analyzing—along with a healthy dose of hypothesizing.

One of those topics is raising a teenager. Am I pressing in on the right things? Am I focusing too much on the stuff that won't make a whit of difference in his life? Does he feel loved by his family and his friends? Does he feel like he can be himself at home? Will we regret that we let him start watching *Saturday Night Live* when he was eleven? Is his faith steady and strong enough to withstand whatever he faces over the next few years? Will his first college roommate move out midway through freshman year because his socks smell like a combination of mildew and Fritos? Will he be forever scarred because of the morning I told him I was leaving for school with or without him at 6:55, then LEFT HIM AT HOME, and then, at 6:56, when I was driving down our street and he called me to make the argument that the oven clock in our kitchen said it was 6:55, my response was, "OH, I AM ON APPLE TIME, SO BYE"?

You can understand my concerns.

And while it might be sort of obvious, I think about relationships between women a whole heck of a lot. This is no doubt related to the work I do at my school, work where I'm charged to encourage our female students to love one another well and walk confidently in who the Lord has made them to be. So given that, how do we work through our differences? How can we honor one another? How do we fight against comparison and learn to rest in contentment? How do we empower one another in Jesus' name to resist the urges to disqualify ourselves, sit back, and watch other people get their hands dirty when we're living in a world desperate for some servant-hearted folks to stand all the way up and lead?

And come to think of it, that leads us to the topic I've thought about more than any other over the last few years.

Leadership.

Oh, I know. *Super* sexy, right?

But oh my goodness—I think about it all the time.

When I was growing up, my hometown hosted an annual event called The Lively Arts Festival. I'm not sure what specifically about the arts was viewed as "lively," but it was always fun to hear what musical acts would be coming to town because Mama and Daddy usually bought tickets. For them this was an uncharacteristic indulgence. Daddy still appreciates a budget more than anybody I know, but if he was going to splurge on anything when I was younger, it was probably going to be season tickets for Mississippi State football or tickets to some sort of live musical performance.

I continue to adore both of these activities. Go figure.

So one or two nights during the week of the Lively Arts Festival, I'd let Mama fix my hair, and I'd put on a sundress or a church dress. Daddy usually opted for a sport coat and his preferred Sansabelt slacks (the early '80s were fancy), and Mama would wear some fab skirt and sweater combo. We'd climb into Mama's Ford LTD, drive downtown, and after we arrived at the restored theatre in my hometown—a venue so old that silent movies showed there back in the 1920s—we'd settle into our seats. For however long the concert lasted, we'd be capti-vated—transported, even—by the performances on that stage.

One year we saw Doc Severinsen, the leader of Johnny Carson's *Tonight Show* band. Another time we saw Marilyn McCoo and Billy Davis, Jr. Another year Steve Lawrence and Eydie Gorme came to town. Between the Lively Arts Festival and a country music festival that our town hosted, there was no shortage of live performances: Lee Greenwood, Ricky Skaggs, Charlie Pride—and there was even a year when we got to see Tony Bennett.

I couldn't have put words to why it all mattered so much at the time, but I can see parts of those nights in my mind as clearly as if they happened this morning. There was a sense of expectation that rippled through the audience; everyone in their Saturday night finest, everyone thrilled to bear witness to such high levels of talent right there in the Piney Woods of Mississippi. And while I have no idea what troubles or pressures weighed heavily on my parents' minds—it was the early '80s, after all, and sharing deep-down concerns just wasn't our family vibe—I do know this: on those nights we sat in the Temple Theatre, those nights with hot pink and bright blue lights illuminating the stage, those nights with Daddy's sport coat draped over the back of his chair and his arm draped around Mama's shoulders, you could look in any single direction and see joy all over people's faces. Contentment. Wonder. Hope.

Those nights at the Temple Theatre didn't change anybody's circumstances.

But I'll bet you anything that they changed some people's perspectives.

I'll bet you anything that they lightened some loads.

I thought about all of this the other night when I was reading an interview with country music artist Eric Church in *Rolling Stone* magazine. I've never met Eric Church, of course, but I could tell within a few paragraphs that he and I have been thinking through some of the same topics. He mentioned to the interviewer that we have a communication problem in our country, that "we dig in, we don't listen and we don't talk."

And what he said next—well, it's stuck with me for the better part of four days. "At a concert," he said, "we all are unified."

Then he finished his sentence: "we all pull on the rope in one way."[1]

Given the current tone of our national discourse, doesn't that sound almost dreamy? Like it might be too good to be true? And to be clear, I don't think our collective unwillingness to listen to one another is because we're cold-hearted. I don't think it's because we enjoy being so divided.

I think, in part, it's because we're afraid. Maybe we're either scared that things will never change, or maybe we're scared that things will never stop changing.

But since folks are busy blaming and calling each other names and finding new and inventive reasons to be outraged (meanwhile doing precious little to build consensus or bridge the gaps), the end result is a bunch of angry people who are sitting around, shouting, unwilling to budge, and unable to see that fear*—big, booming fear, oftentimes pouring out of the mouths of people who are charged to lead us, of all things—has many of us bound up so tight that we probably couldn't move in the same direction even if we wanted to.

Something has to give, y'all.

There has to be a better way.

(*Fear, for the record, is a garbage leadership strategy.)

(*Arrogance masking as confidence is a close second.)

(*And if fear and arrogance are the primary tools in someone's leadership toolkit, we'll do well to find someone else to follow.)

(*Good talk.)

The book of Luke is one of my favorites in Scripture. I certainly don't mean to hurt the feelings of, say, Habakkuk or, you know, Philemon, but Luke is really special to me. Maybe that's because, in Luke, we see the full scope of Jesus' life. We see the moment God broke His 400-year silence when Gabriel foretold the birth of John the Baptist, then appeared again six months later to foretell the birth of Jesus. We see the heartache of Jesus' death, followed by the glory of His resurrection and ascension.

Luke also shows us much about how Jesus lived and led, and it's safe to say that He set a high bar. Because over and over again—without fail, without compromise, without exception—Jesus led from love.

So as we look at the book of Luke, we see the most beautiful picture of Jesus' leadership: the preaching, the healing, the truth-telling, the parable-ing (totally a word), the loving, the challenging, the serving, the feeding, the cautioning, the calming, the blessing, the discipling, the saving, and the sending.

There are also things we *don't* see from Jesus in the book of Luke or in any of the Gospels that chronicle His time on earth: no bragging, no insulting, no demeaning, no belittling, no shaming, no manipulating, no deflecting, no side-stepping, no power-grabbing, no self-protecting, no people-pleasing, no self-obsessing, no self-promoting, and no fear-mongering.

So there's that.

In Luke 8:22, Jesus got in a boat with His disciples and uttered a simple command: "Let us go across to the other side of the lake" (ESV). It's a clear directive, and the disciples heeded it. But somewhere along the way, a storm hit, and their boat began to take on water. Jesus was asleep, His rest seemingly undisturbed by the wind and the waves, but the disciples panicked. They were in danger, so they went to Jesus, woke Him up, and let Him know that they were afraid.

His response? He calmed the wind and the waves. Apparently when Jesus says, "Let us go across to the other side of the lake," you can rest easy in terms of knowing that *He's going to make sure you make it to the other side of the lake.* The disciples, in their fear, forgot that part. They could only focus on the turmoil, but Jesus was both willing and able to still the raging sea—and He would get them to the other side.

When I read this passage a few months ago, I was struck by the miracle, but I was equally struck by the disciples' reaction after Jesus stopped the storm. "Who then is this?" they asked. The disciples—men who had walked and served with Jesus, who had seen Him heal the sick and raise the dead—were incredulous that He was able to do what He did. Their reaction, their "Who then is this?" initially made me think that they had been quick to forget the power of the One who charged them to go in the first place.

However, the more I read and re-read, the more I began to wonder if their reaction was more like astonishment at the depth of Jesus' power, more of a *HEY. Y'ALL. THIS GUY. WE THOUGHT THE HEALING STUFF WAS A BIG DEAL, BUT HE CAN EVEN CALM THIS DARK, VIOLENT SEA.*

Now please understand: I know that not one of us is Jesus. I realize that if any of us are trapped on a boat in the middle of a storm, we may have to use *other gifts* in that crisis because we won't be able to command the waves to stop. But as we lead in our normal, everyday lives—as we steward whatever influence the Lord has given us in the places we live and work and love—what are we doing to calm the storms? To take care of people? To bring order to chaos and peace to confusion? To challenge people in loving ways (Jesus even asked the disciples "Why are you afraid, you of little faith?") and ultimately provide "great calm"?

Because the One who does this?

This is the Jesus of the Gospels.

So here's what I'm asking myself: Am I willing to be an agent of calm in the chaos, or would I rather stir the waters? In short, am I willing to lead like Jesus? Am I willing to follow someone who leads like Jesus? Or on some level do I just want to scream at the waves?

Because we can get in the boat over and over again. We can even fight like crazy to get to where we think we want to go. But apart from Him—apart from His guidance and His comfort and His miraculous peace in the middle of the storms—the waves will continue to throw us around.

We'll continue to flail in fear.

And at some point—inevitably—we'll meet the same fate the disciples would have without Jesus' miraculous intervention.

We'll be dangerously adrift, trapped in the turmoil of the violent sea.

So here's what I want to remember: the disciples may not have known the extent of Jesus's power, but we do.

"Who then is this?"

The One who is always worth following.

The One who calms the storms.

The One whose grace and mercy will enable us to get exactly where He wants us to go.

———•———

One of my favorite developments of the last few years is that Alex and I have discovered we like a lot of the same music. And while I don't want to make a bigger deal of it than it is, I can tell you that shared musical taste might well be all I've ever needed out of motherhood. Forget all of that business about shaping and molding young minds, because my question for you is HOW WILL THE YOUNG PEOPLE KNOW ABOUT GEORGE MICHAEL AND "FREEDOM '90" UNLESS WE TELL THEM?

Just look away if you feel that I've failed.

This whole thing where Alex and I love the same music has been the source of untold volumes of joy. Lately we've been listening to the Billy Joel Channel whenever we're in the car, which has led to the most unexpected blending of my childhood musical memories with the new memories I'm making with my man-child. For those of you who are currently participating in the seemingly endless marathon that is caring for an infant and/or toddler, you need to know that of all the parts of motherhood, this teenager-who-likes-the-same-music deal might well be the best. Because Alex doesn't even roll his eyes when I feel the need to analyze some lyrics, and the only response that seems adequate is some sort of psalm or spiritual song.

I AM NOT EVEN KIDDING.

Every single day is a new musical adventure. Sometimes we listen to Queen and scream-sing "Somebody to Love" on the way home from football practice. Sometimes we ride to school in near silence while John Mayer serenades us with "Dear Marie." Sometimes we take a road trip to Mississippi and attempt to rap our way through the *Hamilton* cast recording. And in the case of this past summer, sometimes we listen to Ben Rector's latest album every single day for about six weeks straight and learn all the lyrics together.

It was a bit of a bonding experience.

So as soon as I found out that Ben Rector was planning a November concert here in Birmingham, getting tickets for that show became a priority. I was thrilled when a friend (hey, Joel) passed along a pre-sale code, and when I relayed the news to Alex that we were going to see Ben Rector live and in person, we both decided that November 1st couldn't get here fast enough.

And you know what? It actually didn't get here fast enough. We felt like we waited on November 1st for about nine years.

We are not what you might call "a patient people."

The night of the concert we arrived at the Alabama Theatre a solid forty-five minutes before showtime. It had been a crazy day, one of those where I wondered if a night at home in pajamas might be a better antidote to the stress that had settled in the pit of my stomach, but Alex's enthusiasm convinced me to stick with the original plan. We found our seats, and Alex headed straight for the merch line. I, on the other hand, sat happily in my seat while I caught up on Instagram and Twitter. David wasn't with us since I declared early on that the concert would be a fun Mother/Son outing, not to mention that the show's 8 o'clock start was incompatible with Papaw's sleeping schedule (he likes to be all the way in the bed by about 8:45). Eventually our friends the Coonses arrived, and we arranged our seating to accommodate the kids: Stephanie and Joey sat beside me, and Alex sat with their daughter Ella—one of his closest friends—on the row right behind us.

This adjustment worked out really well for Ella and Alex because they could pretend not to know us if we sang or danced or moved or breathed in any way that was potentially embarrassing to them.

And I trust you know that we had every intention of BREAKING IT ON DOWN.

Right at eight the opening act came on stage, and as Birmingham audiences are so kind to do, the crowd supported them and cheered them on. Intermission seemed to last forever, but at exactly 9 o'clock, the house lights went down, the stage lights went up, and Ben Rector started to sing.

I think it's safe to say that from the front row to the back row of that theatre—from the floor level to the second balcony—the audience was captivated. And from the opening song to the closing one, we all sang just like somebody had asked us to. We laughed and we "awwwww"'d and we swayed and we clapped. We even followed instructions a few times.

It was magical.

And about halfway through the show, as our fearless leader/singer/songwriter Ben Rector sat at the piano and sang "Sometimes," I choked back unexpected tears for the most unexpected reason. *He wasn't afraid to do something beautiful,* I thought. *He showed up, and he invited us to join him, and now we've all gotten to be a part something really beautiful.*

It was an evening completely devoid of cynicism or bitterness or anger.

It was an evening overflowing with hope.

I was shocked by how much I needed it—and by how much I had missed it.

It was just like Eric Church said: we were all pulling the rope in the same direction. For those ninety minutes, we were united, and Ben Rector called every single one of us to something higher and better.

He called us to something beautiful.

And for an hour and a half, as we all shared space in that 2,500-seat theatre (not exactly a boat, but stay with me), I would even go so far as to say he stilled some storms.

Now. Clearly. Ben Rector isn't Jesus. And music can't save us. I know that. Neither can comedy or art or a non-fiction book of funny-ish essays by a middle-aged woman who lives in the southeastern part of Birmingham.

But maybe we look for opportunities to get in the boat together and remind each other that, as my friend Jamie said recently, we love one another—and we love the Lord—more than we love screaming at the waves. Maybe we take whatever God-given creativity we have and lead with that, pouring it out like an offering. And maybe that offering—that tiny bit of Jesus in us—will start to calm the wind and the waves in our immediate vicinity.

Maybe it's the optimist in me. Who knows. But I do know this: wherever we gather with one another—whether it's in church or at a Ben Rector concert or in the frozen foods section of Trader Joe's—we have an opportunity to lead one another, to serve one another, to encourage one another, to listen to one another, to pull the rope in the direction of Jesus, to walk toward truth, hope, humility, justice, and freedom.

By His grace, we can be a part of something beautiful in the midst of the chaos.

The world screams. Jesus calms.

"Who then is this?"

The only Way forward.

Lord willing, we will lead as we follow Him.

He will get us to the other side.

CHAPTER 11

Served with Love and a Side of Heat Stroke

I've never been one of those people who longs to live in a different time period. For one thing, I really like now. What a time to be alive, you know? We can travel with ease, we can communicate with ease, we can explore different cultures with ease, and sure, maybe I'm making you think that more than anything else, I like me some ease. But I promise it's not just that. It's that I tend to operate from the perspective that right here, right now, is where I'm meant to be, and man am I ever glad that my "right now" happens to coincide with the golden age of television and also Netflix. We thank You, Lord, for these and all Thy gifts.

I have friends, however, who romanticize life in other eras. My cousin Paige, for example, has long wished that she could experience life in the 1800s for even one day. My friend Melanie feels great fondness for the days of Laura Ingalls Wilder, and to tell you the truth I don't even know what decade (or century, for that matter) that is because I was never really able to get past the long dresses and petticoats and aprons (I do not believe that spandex and/or yoga pants were available at the little house or on the prairie). Another friend often mentions how cool it would be to live in the 1920s, and my response is always, "Have you read *The Great Gatsby*? Because that might be the most miserable group of people ever assembled." Plus, the houses weren't air-conditioned, the trains weren't air-conditioned, and even though Jay Gatsby seemed to have more money than Croesus, there wasn't one thing he could do about summertime except to ride it out and sweat like a pig.

Do the Charleston all you want, Gatsby-lovers. I'll be sitting over here on an ice block.

Honestly, the lack of air-conditioning concerns me more than it should when I think about Days of Yore. Because while yes, I admire the selfless, magnanimous deeds—the pioneering acts of progress, if you will—from Ye Olden Days, I can only ponder their significance for about 2.6 seconds before I wonder what the situation was with the weather. I realize that this tendency is, you know, *stupid* on my part, but it's a real thing with me. This means that I can be reading or watching a moving account of Some Historical Instance, and within seconds I've projected my personal cooling requirements onto people who are universally regarded as heroes.

Paul Revere? Burning slap up on the back of that horse.

Ruth and Naomi? Hot as fire walking all the way from Moab to Judah.

Martin Luther? Sweating like a (holy) pig underneath his robes as he nailed the 95 Theses to the church door.

And trust me: it's not just imagined historical scenarios that give me anxiety about the heat. My actual real life has taught me over and over again that I am a kinder, more compassionate human being when I have access to a functioning thermostat. Does this make me superficial and soft? Of course it does. But if you had been with me recently when David and I were riding a New York City subway car where there was only a suggestion of warm-ish air emanating from the vents, you would know for sure that my shadow self emerges with a vengeance in un-air-conditioned environments.

The only positive thing I can say about my behavior that afternoon is that I didn't raise my arms like claws and then hiss at my fellow passengers.

Well.

Several months ago, my boss/principal, Shawn, suggested that we extend our annual senior retreat—which had traditionally been one night away at a camp a few miles outside Birmingham—to two nights away at a camp near the Ocoee River in Tennessee. The camp was rustic, he said, but in addition to the fact that the kids would be able to go white water rafting, the extra time away would hopefully be even more meaningful for our seniors.

I was totally on board. And a few weeks later, when my coworker Bryan asked my friend Heather and me if we'd be willing to serve as "camp cooks" and stay in the air-conditioned (!!!) Cooks' Cabin, I responded with an enthusiastic "yes" before I thought through a single logistical concern. After all, I love to cook, I love to serve teenagers, I love my friend Heather, and I love air-conditioning, especially in August.

This senior retreat idea was getting better and better!

Heather and I had a couple of conversations about what we might serve the kids, but for the most part the late spring / early summer months floated by without much thought about camp or cooking. You might call this "procrastination," but I call it "tucking away the concerns of the inevitable" because that sounds way less negligent. Plus, I did an impressive amount of binge watching in early July, and it proved to be a commitment that didn't leave much room for other obligations and pursuits. How could I possibly think about senior retreat meals when I was busy plowing through season four of a British mystery series I was fairly confident I had already watched? LEAVE ME BE, RESPONSIBILITY.

In late July, though, Heather, Bryan, and I met for a planning lunch. Heather and I had some new ideas about food that might work for the 150 folks we'd be serving, and after we finalized our menus for a Saturday night meal, three meals on Sunday, and Monday morning's breakfast, I offered to make a grocery list that we could review and finalize the next week. Since the camp was only accessible by dirt road or river, we needed to be on point with our list-making and shopping; there would be no quick trips to pick up whatever we forgot to buy.

I've written some long documents in my time—a few books, even—but I can't think of a written document that intimidated me quite like that giant grocery list did. Every day it seemed to morph and expand, not to mention that figuring out how much of everything we needed hurt my math-resistant brain. Heather and I edited and recalculated and added—even going so far as to implement a color-coding system, a level of organization that quite frankly leaves me itchy. Precision has never been my personal superpower, but unlike the twenty-something version of me that would have picked up sixteen boxes of Eggos and called it a cooking day before I blamed the seniors that they didn't have enough to eat, I really wanted to get that grocery list right. For three consecutive nights, I studied it like I was getting ready for a final.

The Wednesday before we left for camp, Heather and I—armed with our encyclopedic list—went to Costco here in Birmingham. It only took us about an hour to round up our non-perishables, and after we dropped off everything at school so it could ride to camp in a Penske truck, I headed to Walmart to grab a few items that Costco didn't have. Our budget was pretty tight, so in addition to trying to make our best guesses about quantities, we also had to mind our nickels. I certainly didn't want to check out at the Costco in Chattanooga—where we planned to buy all of our meat, produce, and dairy—and discover that we were over budget by hundreds of dollars, so I had checked meat prices earlier in the week and nixed the idea of picking up pulled pork at a restaurant in favor of cooking ten well-sized Boston butts ourselves.

Cooking our own pork was going to cost a third as much as buying it from a restaurant. Those butts were a no-brainer.

Much like my own.

I don't even know what that means.

Basically the grocery shopping was an endless installment of *The Price Is Right*, an into-infinity Showcase Showdown where my primary objective in life was to estimate our costs without going over. And by the time we arrived at a Costco outside of Chattanooga on Friday morning, I was focused, I was determined, and I was also trying desperately to block out a vital piece of information Bryan had shared with me a couple of days before.

The camp kitchen wasn't air-conditioned.

Oh, you heard me.

It's totally fair if you're wondering what I did to make Bryan hate me.

So simmering underneath all our calculations was some low- to mid-level anxiety about what our cooking conditions would be. It was, after all, August, so while I felt like we'd land somewhere between "miserable" and "certain death," I was trying to be optimistic. Plus, I wasn't ruling out the option of dragging a table into the walk-in cooler and doing most of my food prep there.

I don't even care if you mock me for that.

———————

It didn't take long for things to get comical after Heather and I (plus our two carts) walked into Costco. Our first stop was the fruit—including cantaloupe, which other people seem to like but I find to be the cardboard of melons—and produce was next. After we selected all of the vegetables, our carts were already halfway full. Somehow, though, our carts seemed to expand to hold everything we needed: an obscene amount of meat, butter, eggs, sour cream, cottage cheese, Italian bread, bacon (I mean, have we met?), and SO. MUCH. CHEESE.

No lie. People straight-up stared.

By the time we left the store's refrigerated sections, our buggies were overflowing, and we needed an extra wide turn radius to get enough momentum to move our carts from one aisle to the next. We paused in the pantry section, and out of the corner of my eye, I spotted something called Johnny's Garlic Spread. I pointed it out to Heather, and as we were debating the pros and cons of using it for garlic bread, an older woman wheeled up beside us and joined our conversation.

"Listen," she said, her voice deep and gravelly. "I don't know what you think you might need that for, but YES. It is phenomenal."

"Really?" Heather answered. "We need to make a whole lot of garlic bread, so we were thinking—"

"Honey," the woman interrupted, "you cannot go wrong with this. You can't. We eat it on everything but ice cream."

Heather's eyes widened as she quickly wedged a jar of Johnny's Garlic Spread into the front of her cart. And as we said our goodbyes,

I told our Garlic Spread Guardian Angel that she needed to make sure to collect her commission from the Costco folks before she left.

Ninety minutes after we began, Heather and I nudged our carts into a checkout line. I was convinced we had gone way over budget—despite the fact that I had done my English-major best to keep a running total as we shopped—and I was a smidge nervous as the cashier rang up our bounty. When she was about to hit the "total" button, I stared at the register display like it was about to reveal all the secrets of life and godliness. Surprisingly, the number was about $300 below our budget, and I legitimately felt like I won a prize. I haven't come that close to performing a herky in a public space since I was fifteen years old.

Loading the car took Heather every bit of a half hour. Oh, I tried to get in there and arrange some things, but it was obvious from the get-go that Heather was our fearless loading leader. I mostly held stuff and repeated encouraging phrases: "That looks great!" "You've got this!" "I've turned on the air!" By the time Heather jammed the last pineapple between the ceiling and a carton of grapes, the back of my car was only about four inches off the ground.

Next stop: our un-air-conditioned camp kitchen paradise.

Around 5 o'clock we pulled into camp and found the dining hall so we could give ourselves a quick tour of the kitchen. It was bigger than we expected—beautifully equipped, in fact. Apart from the fact that there was no air-conditioning, we felt like we had more than what we needed in terms of kitchen equipment, and we were just about to unload my car when the camp caretaker walked in and introduced himself.

His name was Mike, and in addition to being kind, he was thorough. He showed us how to turn on and off every piece of equipment in that kitchen (including the window fans, blessed be the name), and he also introduced us to a feature we missed on our self-guided tour: the walk-in cooler. It was a big space—6 feet wide and 10 feet long—and there was an even larger walk-in freezer behind it. As someone who was on day three of Ever-Present Dread about the heat we'd be dealing with in that kitchen, the cooler/freezer situation was the Lord's assurance to me that the heat would not win the battle. If necessary I could immerse myself in my own personal Arendelle, and I wasn't above dressing in all blue and going full-on Elsa while I chopped fruit to my heart's content in the sub-Arctic comfort of the walk-in freezer.

The cold never bothered me anyway.

Heather and I unloaded the car without too much incident, and as soon as we put everything away and I had found a place for my trusty Bluetooth speaker, we got after it. Heather started working on her breakfast quiches and hash brown casseroles for Sunday morning, and I started working on the lasagna for Saturday night. We had brought our favorite knives from home, along with a few other gadgets that made working in a strange kitchen a little more familiar.

It hasn't been the norm for Heather and me to feed large crowds together, but from the moment we agreed to do the senior retreat cooking, I knew that between the two of us, we could handle it. We've known each other for over ten years; her sweet husband was Alex's first soccer coach, and for the next three of four years we'd run into each other at Homecoming parades and soccer evaluations and basketball camps. Heather's daughter is roughly the same age as Alex, and her son is a couple of years older, so whenever I needed info on summer activities or fifth grade football or what does taking advanced math in 6th grade even mean, Heather was my go-to source. She's as gracious as the day is long, and she also happens to be one of the smartest people I know. About five years ago we became coworkers—she's the Dean of Academics at our school—and during those five years of school days, we have shared hundreds of lunches, solved a slew of the world's problems, and shed more than a few tears as we've walked through the struggles of real-live life. We never seem to tire of analyzing the topics that endlessly fascinate us: Southern writers, small towns, modern-day politics, Southern culture, John Mayer, NEEDTOBREATHE, family dynamics, and Jesus.

Not necessarily in that order.

Our friendship, more than anything else, has been effortless. I've never felt like I needed to work at it or designate time for it. It's low-maintenance, low-drama, and low-pressure. I don't think we've ever had a cross word, though we've apologized to one another on at least 472 occasions when we've felt like we've been short or harsh or rant-y or negative. Then there's this: Heather reminds me so much of my cousin Paige that it's eerie. And honestly, I think that's one reason why our friendship has been so easy. It's like I've known her all my life.

So given our dynamic, it didn't take long for Heather and me to settle into a rhythm as we prepped and browned and stirred and assembled. The combination of window fans and a setting sun made the kitchen less stifling than it could have been (though I do want to go on the record and affirm that IT WAS NOT COOL). So we worked, and we visited, and we abandoned conversations mid-stream only to pick them up again thirty or forty-five minutes later. I quoted my mama *ad nauseum*. We talked about our grandmothers and mar-riage and church. Heather cooked sausage for what seemed like three hours, and I stirred the ricotta / cottage cheese mixture for lasagna until I thought my arm would fall off. Gradually—very, very gradu-ally—we started to make some progress.

By the end of the night, we'd added an assortment of 13 x 20 foil pans to the cooler: lasagnas, breakfast quiches, hash brown casseroles, and marinating Boston butts—two to a pan—each one slathered in dry rub, nested in onions, and topped with a light layer of barbecue sauce. We washed our dishes, wiped down the kitchen, and around 1:00 in the morning, we closed up the kitchen and walked to our cabin.

One day down. Two more to go.

As promised our cabin was air-conditioned; there was a window unit in the front room and a window unit in the bunk room. I wouldn't say that either window unit was *powerful*, exactly, but between the oscillating tower fan we'd hauled from Birmingham and a smaller fan that I aimed at my face, the room where we slept was comfortable. Heather and I each claimed a bottom bunk, and after my shower, I stretched out on the foam mattress and let the muscles in my back and legs scream at me for a little while. Eventually I rolled over on my side in an attempt to stretch my hips, and I read for an hour or so while I waited to fall asleep. I expected to get in the bed and practically pass out, but I was keyed up from the night's activities. It was a problematic development considering that we were planning to wake up bright and early.

⚬━━━━

I didn't actually wake up bright and early.

Well, I mean, I heard my alarm bright and early. But I turned it off. There were several reasons for this decision: 1) my feet—specifically my arches—were very angry about all the standing time from the day before, 2) my eyes felt like they were on fire, and 3) my body was completely unwilling to move in any sort of vertical manner. So

I rolled over, slept for two more hours, and when I finally woke up, I noticed that Heather's bunk was empty. Clearly she had clearly elected to be the responsible one and get to the kitchen.

I winced when my feet hit the floor.

Within ten minutes, though, I was back in the kitchen, knife in hand. Heather had put the pork in the oven about an hour earlier, so the kitchen smelled like really good things were happening. It was humid outside but not super sunny, so I dragged a stool in the direct path of a window fan, grabbed all the ingredients I needed for brownies, and got to work.

The farther we got into the day, the hotter the kitchen was, and I developed a pattern of working for twenty-five or thirty minutes, then walking back to the cooler and standing in the frigid air a minute or two. We were using all the ovens, and when Heather started making what I referred to as her small batch sweet tea (seriously—she made it pitcher by pitcher—little bit by little bit—because it was too hard to pour boiling water from a giant pot), the stove was cranked up too. I had pulled back my hair with a very unattractive black headband early in the day, and by four-ish, when we pulled the pork from the ovens, increased the temperature, and started cooking the lasagna, I was a five-foot-six-inch tower of sweat. Not even the walk-in freezer could relieve the level of heat in that kitchen, and as kids and faculty members started to arrive—they were boating in to camp after spending the day white water rafting—I knew that I *should* be embarrassed by how I looked, but I couldn't muster the will to care.

Welcome, everyone! Don't be alarmed! I don't think you can *actually* sweat to death, but as you can tell, I am giving it my best effort!

So we were burning up, and the kitchen was burning up, and we needed to get those lasagnas out of the oven so they wouldn't be burning up. I turned on a warming cabinet, grabbed two oven mitts, and flung open the oven doors. As quickly as I could—almost like I was in some demented race against myself—I yanked the pans of lasagna from the oven, pivoted 180 degrees, and slid the pans into the warming cabinet. I did this twelve times, and when I finished, I turned down the ovens for Heather's bread. My feet were killing me, so I hobbled to the walk-in, and for the next three-ish minutes, I stood in the center of that chilly oasis and tried to pretend I was cold.

By 5:30, supper was ready, and the next hour was a blur: the kids served themselves salad and bread, and Heather and a couple of faculty members served the lasagna. I was the kitchen runner—replacing empty pans, grabbing lasagnas from the warmer, searching for better lasagna-dispensing utensils, peeling brownies off the parchment paper that was doing its best to hold them captive. The seniors truly could not have been more appreciative, and for about six seconds, Heather and I basked in the glow of how worthwhile our hard work had been.

Then we remembered that we'd be serving three meals on Sunday.

Never say we haven't suffered for you, seniors.

About ten seniors washed, dried, and put away dishes as Heather and I began prep work for the next day's meals, and several of our faculty friends ambled into the kitchen. Some wanted ice, some wanted to talk, some wanted to help, and some simply wanted to stand in the walk-in cooler.

I was so in touch with that last option.

What became immediately clear to me, though, was that time passed so much more quickly while we talked with our friends. I moved from shredding chicken to browning ground beef, and Heather was working on the crust for what she didn't know would be ill-fated lemon squares. Nonetheless, everybody who passed through the kitchen that night lightened our load. We laughed, we problem-solved, and we continued to battle the heat—but we did it with our brothers and sisters by our side.

Now granted, I still went back to that cooler every now and again and asked the Lord to deliver me.

But the company of our friends—their support, their encouragement, their kindness—it was a game changer.

Heather and I walked back to our cabin after midnight, and my whole body hurt just as much as it had the night before.

My heart, however, was twice as full.

It was a little before 6:00 when Heather and I walked into the kitchen Sunday morning. We had done our best to prep for breakfast, but we still had to cook quiches and casseroles and biscuits. Shawn joined us around 6:30, and as Heather and I pulled what we needed from the cooler, he jumped in to help. Some of the girls who were scheduled to set up for breakfast showed up about thirty minutes early—we could not get over how eager they were to help—and before long it felt like we were in my Mamaw Davis's kitchen, brewing coffee and laying out biscuits and setting the buffet for a big family meal.

I had wondered if the kids would eat much breakfast, but I shouldn't have. They loaded their plates with quiche and hash brown casserole and fruit and biscuits—some of them coming back for thirds on those biscuits. They did the same thing at lunch when we fed them pulled pork sandwiches with yummy, super-thick Kettle potato chips and a salad bar complete with Heather's homemade Ranch dressing, all accompanied by sweet tea and gallons of lemonade. They did the same thing at supper when we offered them tortilla chips and tortillas and black beans and corn and chicken and ground beef and cheese and salsa and lo, even more Ranch dressing and sweet tea. Every single meal they surprised us with their appetites and their enthusiasm and their gratitude. Every single meal they made us forget about the heat and the sweat and the aching feet—because every single meal they helped us remember that when we serve one another in love, the ties that bind us just get stronger.

After Sunday night's supper we gathered—all 150 of us—at an amphitheater area near the water. The amphitheater was about half a mile from our cabin, so I drove my car, as is my middle-aged privilege (my hips, y'all—they had back-talked me all dadgum day). We sang a few worship songs before Shawn shared a message, and afterward, several kids stood up to cast a vision for their senior year.

Their leadership in that moment encouraged and humbled me. It reminded me of something too.

As excited as I was about going out of town for senior retreat, when I realized that it was the last weekend before school started—my last chance for several months to write at my pace and on my time before the demands of the school year set in—there was a part of me that resented the imposition. Maybe, now that I think about it, that was the heart of my senior retreat humbling: if anything is motivating us more than esteeming and loving and caring for the people in our all-the-way-real-lives—do our timelines and schedules and objectives really matter that much after all?

We're not always aware of it, but we often speak a language of upward mobility—especially with the younger people in our lives. From an early age we challenge them to move up, get ahead, and shoot for the stars. As adults we hang pictures of mountains in our offices to remind us to keep striving for the summit, and we equate success with being at the top of the heap as opposed to the bottom of the barrel.

In Scripture, however, we see a markedly different standard. Because in Scripture, we're frequently reminded of the power of living low. Jesus' final meal with His disciples is a prime example.

For starters, it's almost impossible to read John's account of the Last Supper (John 13) without thinking about what was weighing on Jesus' heart and mind. We learn in verse 1 that "Jesus knew that his hour had come to depart from this world to the Father." And just in case we missed it, John gave us verse 3: "Jesus knew that the Father had given everything into his hands, that he had come from God, and that he was going back to God."

On top of that, Jesus knew that one of His disciples would betray Him.

So I don't want to oversimplify it, but Jesus was dealing with some heavy realities.

And if we look at the Last Supper through the lens of a "climb the ladder" culture, then we might think that Jesus really missed an opportunity with His friends. After all, He was the Son of God—*sort of a big deal*—and it would have been understandable if, at His last meal with the disciples, He sat back, bemoaned His fate, and listened while men who walked so closely with Him showered Him with praise and gratitude.

Instead, though, Jesus got low. In fact, He didn't even finish His meal (v. 4). He laid aside His clothes, tied a towel around His waist, and stooped to wash the feet of His disciples (v. 5).

He could have insisted on being exalted, on receiving adulation, but He chose to serve. To love. To minister. To bend down.

I wish the Lord didn't have to keep reminding me that "this is the way, walk in it" (Isa. 30:21 ESV)—and I wish I understood why my heart is so stubborn in this regard—but far more important than professional productivity or "fulfilling a calling" or "making an impact" is *service*: doing whatever we do so that Jesus will be "high and lifted up" (Isa. 57:15 ESV) and (and!!!) refusing to measure our work's value by any metric other than God's economy. In my case this means that there may be times when I write, times when I sit with heartbroken girls at school, times when I sit on a stool and sweat sort of an embarrassing amount while I sear seventy-five chicken breasts. This is the unglamorous, unheralded, often unnoticed practice of laying down our preferences and priorities for someone else's sake, of putting ourselves in a position where we have no personal agenda, no ulterior motive, and no end game.

And we stand up for each other by getting as low as we possibly can.

I'm convinced that this is the best work there is. This is the kingdom coming.

And these are the days that God has given us—to love, to serve, to bend down, and to make His mercies new and known.

Where else could we possibly want to be?

Yes, senior retreat was hot. Yes, it was exhausting. Yes, it was a sacrifice of time and energy and sleep. Yes, I burned both of my arms because I'm "clumsy" and "can't hold large pans well" and "didn't take long oven mitts with me."

But would I willingly volunteer to cook for those young'uns again?

You'd better believe I would.

Just tell me the date, and I'll be there with a personal spray fan and oven mitts on.

I wouldn't miss it for the world.

CHAPTER 12

Dark Chocolate, YouTube, and the Irresistible Love of the Living God

These days I'm generally reluctant to write about parenthood because, in so many ways, the jury is still out. Plus, you know, I have one whole child, so it's not like I have years of experience with launching exceptional humans into the world. I'm just sort of taking life with our teenager as it comes, and as of right this very second, we still really like him a lot. This gives me some hope.

Another reason why it's tricky to write about parenthood is because the temptation is to construct a highlight reel that reads like the most annoying Facebook post ever because Alex is just so awesome and Alex is just a joy and did I tell you how fantastic Alex is because wow, is he ever fantastic *#53OnTheFootballField #1InOurHearts #Blessed*. So what I have to remember is that my job as a mama isn't to try to construct a reputation for my child. In fact, I frequently remind myself that even Mary and Joseph managed to be level-headed about their son, Jesus—who, by the way, was without any sin at all whatsoever—when it came to the All-Star Kid Awards. How do I know this? Because in Luke 2, when Mary and Joseph dedicated Jesus at the temple and Simeon said that Jesus was "a light for revelation to the Gentiles, and for glory to your people Israel" (v. 32), Mary and Joseph "marveled at what was said about him" (v. 33).

All I'm saying is that if Mary was surprised by what Simeon had to say about her son, then maybe I can calm down when it comes to telling you about how Alex blocked a shot in a lacrosse game. Because if anybody gets to humble-brag about their kid on Facebook, it seems reasonable that we should let Mary move on up to the front of the line. As far as I'm concerned, she can wear out *#Blessed* and the rest of us can stick with *#WorkInProgress* and *#FingersCrossed*.

Because the parenting, it is humbling. And dealing with the children—well, it is an unpredictable business. Yes, we're responsible for teaching them and training them and raising them in the fear and admonition of the Lord, but by the same token I don't think anything or anyone has been more instructive in my life than the six-foot-tall somebody who sleeps a couple of doors down the hall and cannot keep his laundry folded and put away for love nor money.

And that brings us to the thing that I feel more comfortable writing about (because, as I mentioned, when it comes to the parenting piece, THE JURY HAS NOT YET RETURNED A VERDICT): in addition to the teenager living in my house, there are a whole bunch of teenagers I get to hang out with every single day at work. For an obnoxious number of years I was a high school English teacher—which was its own set of delights and joys—but as I've mentioned before, about five years ago I transitioned from the classroom to a job called Dean of Women. It sounds sort of fancy, my title, like I should get to wear a robe or something, but it's actually a super unfancy scenario. I work mainly with our high school girls, and truth be told, I'm as much of a drama coach as anything else (just not the kinds of productions you might see on a stage). Fortunately, our school has wonderful guidance counselors who work with our kids when they face serious issues like depression or self-harm or eating disorders, so I'm more of a sounding board for the daily stresses: trouble with friends, frustration about schoolwork, arguments with boyfriends, and figuring out what faith looks like in the day-to-day. I also deal with dress code referrals, which means that my next book will be a collection of essays entitled *I Have No Patience for the Crop Tops*.

My first few years in the new job were challenging and fun and exhausting and rewarding—full of relationships I will treasure forever even if my voice in most girls' lives is a short-term deal (they go to college, they grow up, they move on, and this is how it should be). And at the beginning of this year, I assumed that it would be another challenging and fun and exhausting and rewarding time, another couple of semesters marked by laughs and tampons (I give out so many tampons) and tears and an obscene amount of Dove Sea Salt Caramel Dark Chocolate.

I wasn't wrong about that.

But what I never expected—what never really occurred to me—was what it would be like to have Alex's grade in the building with me. Of course I love the other grades—I spend lots of time with them and could write a whole chapter about what a gift it has been to get to know our junior girls better this year—but there's something about the combination of Alex's grade with the older grades that has grounded and delighted and challenged me.

I've always loved my job, but this year—well, it has been the biggest blast.

Which makes it all the more weird that lately, I've been wrestling with some work-related questions.

Over Christmas Break I had hoped to finish this book that you're reading right now, but somewhere in between mapping out chapters and typing out words, I wandered into a bit of a YouTube rabbit hole. Obviously, I've watched stuff on YouTube countless times over the course of the last fourteen-ish years (and in the overachieving department, I feel that I am personally responsible for a solid 70 percent of the views of Justin Timberlake and Chris Stapleton's performance at the 2015 CMA Awards, thank you and you're welcome), but I never paid much attention to YouTube's original content.

Well. Suffice it to say that SOME THINGS CHANGED this past Christmas.

It all started with some *Architectural Digest* videos—tours of Ricky Martin's California home and Robert Downey Jr.'s house-that-looks-like-a-windmill in the Hamptons—and after an hour or so of watching various celebrities in various homes situated in various locales, I clicked on a video in the sidebar out of sheer curiosity. The video, which boasted millions of views, featured a young woman who decided to buy every single candle in Bath & Body Works, then scoop a melon baller of wax from each candle, drop it in an industrial-sized boiler, and melt all the scoops together for what she called a "Frankencandle."

That last sentence is one of the strangest things I have ever written.

But listen—in America, YOU CAN DO ANYTHING.

The candle video completely captured my attention (I'm pretty sure that my mouth was hanging open for upwards of fifteen minutes), and a week or so later, with a still-unfinished book but a wealth of new YouTube knowledge, I returned to school. The morning was full of catching up on emails and getting some upcoming events on the calendar, so at lunchtime, when five or six freshman girls asked if they could eat in my office, I was thrilled. I pushed my laptop to the side, pulled out my lunch, and listened to the girls recap their Christmas holidays.

"So then? We went to my GRANDmother's."

"Ohmygosh we also saw that movie, and it was a-MAZE-ing."

"Same! I got those pants from Urban too! SAME SAME SAME!"

Listen, y'all. It's a sociolinguistics lab inside Room 113.

After several minutes one of the girls piped up and said, "SO. Miss Soph. What did you do for Christmas?"

I shared a few details about how we had family in town for a big portion of the break, how we had friends over on New Year's Eve, how it was a bummer when Mississippi State lost their bowl game, and then I threw in some information that apparently bonded us all for life: "And you know what else? I watched a ton of YouTube videos, including one about a girl who melted a whole bunch of Bath & Body Works candles together."

The room went silent before one of the girls spoke up.

"OH MY GOSH MISS SOPHIE. WAS IT A SAFIYA NYGAARD VIDEO? BECAUSE I LOVE HER."

"YASSSSSSSSSSSSSS," echoed the other girls. They were like a YouTube chorus, and every one of them knew about Safiya Nygaard, her candle video, and her entire body of YouTube work.

They then proceeded to rattle off a succession of names I had never heard—other famous YouTubers, I presumed—but I didn't even care that I was clueless. Because for just a second, I felt like I stepped behind the high school girl veil, like I accessed information that they prefer to share among themselves but will only occasionally acknowledge when they're in the company of The Old People.

While it was a little difficult for me to understand, their excitement about Safiya Nygaard was similar to what I might feel if you told me that someone was coming to my house to deliver a custom charcuterie board and also John Mayer would be playing an acoustic guitar house concert in my living room from 6 to 9 and, ONE MORE

THING, I don't have to share the bacon-wrapped dates with anyone while my good friend John sings "Neon."

What I'm telling you is that the girls were elated.

And considering that I've pretty much given up on keeping up with what the kids are enjoying, their enthusiasm was humbling. In fact, just a couple of months before, I was trying to remember the name of a singer Alex and I had been talking about the previous night, but his name wouldn't come to my mind. The singer was Shawn Mendes, but I could not seem to convince my brain to access that particular file of my memory, and no joke—for about fifteen seconds I convinced myself that the singer in question was someone named Brian Chalmers.

Brian Chalmers.

I'm sure you've heard all his hits.

So connecting with the girls about Safiya Nygaard—it was a real win. Because here's the truth of the matter: when you work with teenagers all day long and you're pushing fifty, it's easy to get in your head and think that there's probably someone younger who could relate to them more, serve them better, and interact with them way more effectively.

There's probably someone younger who isn't, you know, next-level excited about the prospect of a really good (imaginary) charcuterie board.

I adore being at school with Alex. I adore being at school with his friends. I get such a kick out of getting to be the tiniest part of our high school kids' lives.

But sometimes, I get in my head about it.

And lately, it seems, it takes me a while to find my way out.

I've said it many times, but Birmingham really is the best of all the cities. I love it so much that whenever I come home from traveling and am driving down Red Mountain Expressway on the way to my house, I will wave at the general downtown area and say, "I love you, Birmingham!" as if it can actually hear me. I am absolutely crazy about it (It's the perfect size! There's so much to do! It's the hidden gem of the South!), and what I know for certain is that the absolute best part of Birmingham is the people. There are a few turkeys, sure, but mostly the people are awesome: friendly, resourceful, and helpful. These are such good things.

Birmingham also has a good-sized creative community, and as a person who writes and podcasts and etc., I'm so grateful to live in a city where there are folks doing similar things. It's been enormously helpful to sit at lunches and dinners and coffees with my friends who are working in creative spaces, mainly because 1) they're all kinds of funny and 2) it saves me a fortune on therapy bills.

About a month ago I met my super creative friends Jamie and Erin for dinner. Jamie co-hosts a couple of podcasts (*The Popcast* and *The Bible Binge*), and Erin produces live shows for *The Popcast* and contributes to *The Bible Binge*. Jamie and Erin are both Instagram delights—seriously two of the funniest, smartest women I know—and spending time with them is always energizing and inspiring. On that particular night we must have sat at our table for two and a half hours while we broke down an absurd number of topics, including but not limited to podcast advertising, audio book ideas, Botox, the wonder of Nivea moisturizing cream (the one from Germany, not the one made in the US; trust me when I tell you that Jamie knows these things), podcasts we love, book contracts, assorted family challenges, and bread pudding. I listened as they talked about what they're planning for this year and what they would like to do down the road. I'm forever fascinated by people whose brains work this way; I am not a planner and tend to err on the side of *oh, it'll all work out*. I don't do much (or any, really) strategic thinking when it comes to the writing, speaking, and podcasting parts of my life because for one thing it makes me a little tired and for another thing I'm really not much of a goal-setter.

So. Be sure to contact me the next time your company needs a productivity expert!

What I love about Jamie and Erin is that their planning is directly connected to their deep desire to serve. This work that they're doing is their ministry, and they want to do it well. I so admire their commitment because for the longest time I've lived in between two worlds—my school world and my creative world—and to be honest, after I've spent a day at school with teenage girls who are talking about boys and periods and Steve Madden sneakers and Urban Outfitters, the last thing I want to do when I get home is promote my books. Or engage with a living soul on social media. Plus, right now I'm on a break from Instagram because the level of self-promotion is making me cuckoo. I totally understand that it's the nature of the social media and publishing business. I also understand that nobody wants to see a picture of me laughing at something off in the distance while I hold a copy of my latest book. Bottom line: I don't care for branding. I'm not a product. And I stink at marketing.

So, you know, there's not a lot of *strategy* happening over here.

And every once in awhile, my lack of intention with the planning and promotion side of things gets to me. Should I be further along with my writing? Should I try to speak more? Should I commit—all the way commit—to focusing on the creative side of my life and leave the school part behind? If I live my life with feet in two different worlds, is either one of those worlds really getting the best of me? Am I missing something? Am I doing this wrong?

As you might imagine, by the time I left my dinner with Jamie and Erin, I was ALL UP IN MY HEAD about these things. They're both so thoughtful about their careers, and I'm just trying to write two or three paragraphs for the next book while I sit in my car at Alex's football practice. They're spending their workdays dreaming up hilarious podcast episodes and clever live show content, and I'm texting Melanie in between dress code referrals to see if we can podcast that afternoon between 3:45 and 5:15—but really I need to leave the house at 4:45 because Alex has a lacrosse game on the other side of town and by the way does she know of anything at all we can talk about when we record.

I bet I wasn't a mile away from the restaurant when I left Melanie a voice message that said, essentially, *Hey, we're doing all of this stuff the wrong way. We need to get our act together. I'm so inspired by Jamie and Erin, and while I can't say exactly what that means for us, I want to do this better. I don't want to waste the opportunity we've been given to do this cool stuff. I know it's harder because I'm at school all day, but I want us to talk about it. I think we can work smarter.*

And then, when I got home, David said, "Hey! How was your dinner?" and I fell apart. I cry about three times a year, but that night, I couldn't stop the tears. Finally I went to sleep—and then I woke up the next morning and cried some more. At lunch I cried with my friend Heather—telling her all the ways that I feel like I'm missing something, wondering if I'm wasting the prime of my writing/speaking life at school, but knowing that at the same time, I love being there. I love those kids so much. I love reminding those kids how deeply Jesus loves them, how perfectly He made them.

I love watching them figure out how to love each other.

Even now—just writing about it—it makes me emotional. Because I've spent over half my life working with high school kids, and it's been enormously fulfilling, never more so than this past year with Alex and his friends in the building with me. But still, I wonder: am I missing something? Is there a part of my creative life that will never be fully realized because the days and months I spend in room 113 keep me from giving this writing/speaking/podcasting thing everything I have?

I mean, I'm not planning to have any pictures made for Instagram while I'm wearing a floral maxi-skirt (barefooted, of course) and holding a copy of *Giddy Up, Eunice*, but should I be putting more effort into that part of my life?

When I talked to Heather that day at lunch, she listened to me for about ten minutes before she said, in the kindest way, "I think you might be believing a lie."

"Okay," I said. I wasn't sure if I wanted to hear what she was going to say next.

Heather went on to tell me, in so many words, that there's not an expiration date on the creative part of my life. Hopefully I still have some years stretching out in front of me, and because she sees me every single day at work and sees me with the kids I serve, she knows the joy I get from those relationships. She knows how much I love being with Alex and his friends. She knows how much I would miss that if I decided to focus more on the strategic sides of podcasting and writing. And she knows how miserable I would be—as someone who hates things like stats and sales figures and spreadsheets—if I was spending my days knee-deep in that stuff, tangled up in the details of trying to make my creative outlets a full-time job.

Without belaboring the point, I'll just say this: she's right.

The following Sunday, I sat down in church, weary from a week of way too much emotion and introspection, and I listened to our pastor introduce Matthew 20:17–38. The mother of Zebedee's sons wanted to make sure that there was a special seat—right next to Jesus—for each of her sons. She wanted prominence for her boys, but after Jesus explained that "to sit at my right and my left is not mine to give; instead it is for those for whom it has been prepared by my Father" (v. 23), He addressed the disciples. He said, ". . . whoever wants to become great among you must be your servant . . . just as the Son of Man did not come to be served, but to serve" (vv. 26, 28).

And while the whole sermon was enormously impactful, I keep looking back at my notes and finding encouragement in three specific points Matt (our pastor) made. These are his words, not mine:

1. God intervenes to keep me from choosing my greatness over His greatness.
2. Servanthood is greatness in the kingdom of God. He loves humility (and then I wrote, "SLOW YOUR ROLL, SOPHIE HUDSON").
3. Don't be afraid of doing the thing in front of you.[2]

It was a timely word.

And over the last few weeks, as I've thought and pondered and prayed, here's what I've realized.

Serving through their creativity is the most natural thing in the world for friends like Erin and Jamie. They're devoting an enormous amount of energy to that part of their lives because *God wants them to devote an enormous amount of energy to that part of their lives*. It is exactly where He has called them.

But right now, for reasons I may never understand this side of heaven, the Lord has me (mostly) with the teenagers. The writing/speaking/podcasting stuff is awesome—I love it a lot—but it's not my primary focus. Outside of home, school is the place in my life that gets the bulk of my service. And here was my biggest post-sermon epiphany: what's turning my head in terms of wondering if I'm missing out on something is FEAR, not conviction.

You know what will get us into a mess? Making decisions out of fear instead of conviction.

So for the time being, at least, I keep a foot in each world.

But school, for better or worse, has a bigger piece of my heart.

And ya girl is good with that.

———

It just occurred to me, but while this last year of work has created some internal conflict, there's something about this particular mix of freshmen, sophomores, juniors, and seniors who roam the high school halls that has made me crazy optimistic about the future. This is ironic, because for most of my time in my current job—especially during and after the circus that the most recent presidential election was for the entire country, regardless of politics or party—I've felt like the world was either burning down, falling apart, or some combination of the two. And as the years progress, and more insanity happens in the political sphere, I'm sure I'll be tempted to feel the same way.

However, despite my best efforts to imitate Chicken Little and warn everyone around me that THE SKY, IT IS FALLING, I have to say: THESE KIDS, y'all.

They're something else. They're perspective-shifters.

Several months ago a few of Alex's closest girlfriends decided that after they wrapped up their JV basketball season, they were going to give JV soccer a try. None of them had played soccer since they were in elementary school, but they thought it would be fun to play another team sport together. So when the basketball season ended, they jumped right in to soccer practice. Last week they had their first game on a rainy, dreary Monday, and oh, the girls were excited.

They weren't far into that first game when Alex's friend Ashby, whose feet were planted on the field, turned to make a play and heard a loud "pop" before she fell to the turf. Initially everyone hoped that maybe she sprained or dislocated her knee, but an MRI showed that her ACL was completely torn. Ashby gives all her effort to whatever she's doing—she loves to compete—so the prospect of surgery, then nine to eleven months of rehab and recovery, left her feeling discouraged and overwhelmed. It's easy to understand why.

So Tuesday night, Alex and I met his friend Charlie (and Charlie's mom, Suzanne) for dinner. The boys, who have played football together since 6th grade, shared so many thoughts and opinions over the course of our meal, and because they're teenagers, they couldn't just nod their heads or say "you're right" when they agreed with each other. Instead, they would utter some variation of "Big facts, bruh" or "That is big facts" or "Facts, bro" to second the other's theories, and by the time we left the restaurant, I felt more bro-tastic than I knew was possible. I didn't give anyone a bro-hug where you pound your right fists and then pat each other's backs with your left hand, but I would have considered playing a quick quarter of tackle football or maybe some light ice hockey.

BIG FACTS, BRUH.

After supper Suzanne went home, and I took the fellas to see Ashby. The hope was that the combination of Starburst FaveReds, hot pink tulips, and a visit with the boys would lift her spirits. When we got to her house, Alex and Charlie plopped down next to her on the sofa, and I sat down in the kitchen to visit with Kasey, Ashby's mom, and our friend Steph, who had also stopped by. Kasey filled us in on some of the plans for surgery and physical therapy, and at some point in our conversation, I looked over in the kids' direction.

All I could see were the backs of their heads. I have no idea what they were talking about, but their body language told a whole story. They were leaning into each other, laughing, Ashby's head turning from Alex to Charlie and back to Alex. I got Kasey's attention and whispered, "Hey. Look at them."

For several seconds we stood there and flat-out stared.

"I'm so grateful," Kasey whispered back to me.

We repeated that routine about five times over the next hour.

At one point Ashby was clearly emotional, and Alex wrapped his arm around her and pulled her toward his chest (this is huge progress, because when they were in 7th grade and something scared Ashby, Alex sort of froze in place and Ash had to say, "Alex! Comfort me!"). A few minutes later Ash rested her head on Charlie's shoulder for about a half-second, and then, almost instantly, everybody was laughing again.

It was a little after nine when we said our good-byes and headed home. But for the rest of the night, I thought about seeing the backs of those three heads while I sat in Kasey's kitchen. And this may sound overly dramatic, but I'm not so sure that I care: as a mama and as someone who gets to love and serve those three kids every day at school, it was a memorial stone moment for me.

Yep. You heard me. Kasey's sectional sofa is my Ebenezer.

Okay not really.

But y'all. IT WAS SUCH A BIG DEAL. And it was such confirmation of why I continue to stay planted in the school world: because every single day I watch teenagers figure out what it means to love one another, to care for one another, and to be the body of Christ when someone is hurt or afraid.

It's such messy work. Especially since, sometimes, teenagers can be real jerks.

So can we.

Sometimes teenagers can get really petty.

So can we.

Sometimes teenagers can prey on one another's fears and manipulate the daylights out of each other.

So can we.

But oh my goodness—when the love of Jesus breaks through? And when these kids we're so crazy about learn to sit in it, rest in it, stand in it, extend it, and sincerely care for one another with it? That, my friends, is a sight to behold.

I want to bear witness to that.

And every single day that I'm in room 113, I *get* to bear witness to that.

So do you—wherever the Lord has called you.

I don't know if you're in an office with a bunch of middle-aged folks, in a pre-school classroom with some feisty four-year-olds, in a playroom with your three kids, in a studio creating content for people who really need your company during a long commute, in front of a spreadsheet making sense of details or someone else's money (bless you), or in a courtroom advocating for someone who is doing her best to cling to some small shred of hope.

But I do know this, no matter where you are.

Serve those people by loving them. Right there. Right where you are. Stand right there with them, right where they are.

Sure, you may have to sit a minute before they're ready to move on or move forward. That's a sweet time, too. But however you're ministering to and serving the people around you, remember that they're not there by accident.

And neither are you.
Neither are any of us.
Stand with them.
Serve them.
After all, that's what Jesus did for us.
And our pesky fears and doubts that try to get in the way?
They've got nothing on Him.

CHAPTER 13

Now Is When We Walk Up the Hill

I'm pretty sure I've written about this before—and if I haven't, then yay, here's a new story for all of us—but when I was growing up, I had a really hard time letting people see my imperfections. Our family wasn't perfect by any stretch of the imagination, but for some reason (oh, I'll go ahead and name it) (insecurity!) I needed for people to think that it was. If I had a weakness—and I had plenty—I wasn't going to talk about it. If my family was struggling in some way, I wasn't going to open up about it during prayer request time at youth group. As far as I was concerned, everybody could think that the Sims family was swimming in a sea of awesome, and if there was any shame or suffering, then I was happy to deal with that in private, far away from the gossip and glares of people who might be tempted to pretend to care.

That was a pretty cynical worldview for a teenager, huh?

And here's the irony: I had lots of friends. It wasn't like I locked myself away in my room and never came out. I just knew how to be selective about what I told people, and now that I've typed that, I realize that it sounds like we were a family full of scandals and secrets.

That wasn't the case at all. In fact, now that I look back, we were pretty stinkin' normal. What we weren't, however, was perfect—and that very real reality didn't follow the script I had written in my head. So I pretended.

I pretended about lots of things, as a matter of fact. I pretended that I knew what it meant to live a life surrendered to Jesus. I pretended that I understood Algebra II when I might as well have been trying to read the Septuagint in Greek. I pretended that a failing test grade probably wouldn't affect my average *that* much. I pretended that my relationships with guys meant more to those guys than they actually did, and I pretended that keeping my problems to myself was a fine way to handle my personal business. One time I even pretended that I didn't cheat on a Spanish test despite the fact that I wrote the vocabulary words on my desk in pen and my teacher had me dead to rights. But I didn't confess, and I didn't deny it; I just walked out of the class like I didn't have a care in the world, and we never talked about it again.

So in addition to some pretending, there was also some lying. And whenever something didn't fit into my preferred narrative for This Is How Life Should Go, I just ignored it, shoved it to the back of my brain, and went on my merry way.

It was incredibly irresponsible.

It was also exhausting.

And while it wasn't comfortable to break out of the pretending—in lots of ways pretending felt like home to me—I eventually did. I attribute my victory in this area to the refining work of the Holy Spirit and also the covenant of Holy Matrimony. Because you know what doesn't work in a marriage? Pretending. There's nowhere to run, nowhere to hide, and you reach a point where you either have to own your personal dysfunction or sit back and be consumed by it. So one day, when my pretending felt to David a lot more like lying (and to be clear, I had lied to him about several things), I sat down in the middle of our kitchen floor, and I owned it. I was mortified for my husband to see me like that—exposed and broken by my own choices—but I also felt relieved. And over time—in the weeks and months and years that followed—I gradually lost the will to pretend. Now, almost twenty years later, I can honestly look back on that day—that fork in the road—and give "done with pretending" two solid thumbs up. 10/10. Highly recommend.

The bigger picture for me, though—and what I was only able to see by looking back at the choices of Younger Me—is that while yes, all that pretending made me isolated and manipulative, it actually had a far bigger consequence: it prevented me from learning how to sincerely and vulnerably ask other people for help. I saw pretending/skipping over the hard stuff as a solution. WHY WASN'T EVERYONE DOING THIS? But man oh man I missed so many opportunities to experience the grace of exposure, the grace of humility, and the grace of admitting my deep need for other people's wisdom, prayers, and guidance.

These days, on the cusp of my fifties, pretending isn't as much of a deal for me. For the most part you don't have to wonder how life is going or what I'm thinking because I will tell you. Good, bad, ugly, or indifferent. But what most definitely *is* a deal for me is the ongoing recognition that God intends for us to be safe places for one another. He intends for us to be vulnerable with one another. He intends for us to stand beside one another. And He intends for us to cry out to one another and to resist the urge to pretend when we're desperate for one another's help.

It's our sacred duty, our charge, as we care for our fellow image-bearers.

Help.

H-E-L-P.

It took me a long time to figure it out, but now? It's one of the most beautiful four-letter words I know.

———

This may feel like a hard left, but we're going to travel back to the Old Testament for a minute.

Specifically, we're going to travel back to the book of Exodus, which means we're going to see Moses doing his best to get the Israelites out of Egypt. Here's what's going on in Exodus 17:9–13:

> *Moses said to Joshua, "Select some men for us and go fight against Amalek. Tomorrow I will stand on the hilltop with God's staff in my hand."*
>
> *Joshua did as Moses had told him, and fought against Amalek, while Moses, Aaron, and Hur went up to the top of the hill. While Moses held up his hand, Israel prevailed, but whenever he put his hand down, Amalek prevailed. When Moses's hands grew heavy, they took a stone and put it under him, and he sat down on it. Then Aaron and Hur supported his hands, one on one side and one on the other so that his hands remained steady until the sun went down. So Joshua defeated Amalek and his army with the sword.*

Now I know I'm normally pretty chatty and prone to chasing a narrative rabbit, but for the sake of not taking sixteen paragraphs to tell you why I think this particular passage is so instructive about how we give and receive help, I'm going to number a few of my initial observations.

BEHOLD THE EFFICIENCY.

1. Moses was God's chosen man to lead the Israelites out of Egypt. He had the staff of God with him, and that staff was a "wonder-working rod which had summoned the plagues of Egypt, and under which Israel had passed out of the house of bondage."[3] Even still, Moses didn't go up that hill alone. Neither should we.

2. Moses took Aaron—who was his brother—and Hur up the hill with him. He knew that he was going to need them, and he knew he could count on them for support. We also need to be wise about who goes up the hill with us. When tough times hit—when we're in a battle—we want people with us who are trustworthy, loving, and loyal. This requires discernment, and Moses had it. Aaron and Hur were his guys.

3. Aaron and Hur could have gotten into a deep conversation and ignored whatever was going on with Moses. They could have given a play-by-play of the battle below them. But instead, they paid attention to the circumstances. The Israelites clearly were in better shape when the staff was raised, so Aaron and Hur focused on supporting Moses. They found a stone for him to sit on, and they raised his arms when he was too weak to hold them up himself. It was exactly what Moses—and by virtue of that, the Israelites—needed at the time. Because don't miss

this: when you help one person, that care will ripple throughout your community.

4. When we love and help our friends without any agenda, it spurs them on just like Moses' staff spurred on the Israelites. The help we offer each other encourages people we don't even know are watching. Maybe you're not fighting the Amalekites, but you might be fighting a war with selfishness, a war with family brokenness, or a war with injustice in your community. If we help each other, we have a better chance for victory.

5. Like Moses, you have a staff. I mean, not a literal one, probably, though if you're into shepherding then consider this sentence a virtual high-five. But you for sure have a God-given something that enables you to lead and serve and help God's people. Maybe it's accounting or teaching or organizing or cooking or compassion or gentleness or patience or singing or whatever. But you have a staff.

Remember that. Please and thank you.

So. Here's the deal: Moses was God's chosen man. He could have easily refused help. He could have pretended all would be well, and he could have gone up that hill alone. On top of that, Aaron and Hur could have ignored Moses' need for help; they could have said, "All righty, Mr. Staff of God—walk up that hill and do your thing. You're God's man, right? Have at it."

But victory required some teamwork.

And this is where I'm convinced—I. AM. CONVINCED.—that we have to do a better job helping each other.

Well, first of all, we have to do a better job *seeing* each other.

And when we see our brothers and our sisters who are fighting for something that matters, we walk up the hill with them. When they're raising the staff, so to speak, as they fight and pray, we come alongside them, just like Aaron and Hur did for Moses. Just like Moses did for Joshua.

And when they're weary, and they're tired, and they're unsteady, we stand beside them. We give them a place to rest. We lift their arms. We fight with them.

For way too long, I was so focused on my own life, my own needs, my own comfort that I neglected to see—much less help in—battles all around me.

But the way it was isn't the way it has to be.

It isn't the way it *should* be.

So you know what?

It's time to walk up some hills.

The last couple of years have been rough for the American church. In fact, if you asked me to give a summary of 2015–now, I would say A GREAT DEAL OF ARGUING. And if you don't believe me, then please let me introduce you to a little something called the Twitter, not to mention that the Facebook has some sights to see as well.

Honestly, this is where I'm tempted to make a comprehensive list of the issues that have divided the church, that have broken our hearts, that have exposed our collective blind spots.

But I'm not sure that's helpful at this point in the discussion—because ultimately I think any list I make would be more likely to create a barrier as opposed to a bridge. You might wonder why I listed this thing and not that thing, or don't I know about the other thing, or wait—do I not even care about the most important thing of all? BECAUSE EVERYBODY KNOWS HOW IMPORTANT THAT THING IS.

So. Let's not get caught up in the weeds; in fact, let's just agree to meet on the Bridge-o-Generalities. I think we're more likely to find common ground that way—a nice, level spot so we hopefully get a better view of the hills all around us.

Because here's what we know: at the base of all those hills, there are battles aplenty. I'm speaking metaphorically, of course, because as far as I know there aren't any people marching around in actual armor and carrying actual swords. But there are culture wars, policy wars, theological wars, political wars, gender wars, philosophical wars, ethical wars, relational wars, and sometimes, as disheartening as it might be, personal wars—Christian vs. Christian, ONE NIGHT ONLY, in a UFC Primetime Battle.

Or, you know, an endless back and forth on social media.

Now—has there also been wonderful stuff going on in the American church? Absolutely. We could cite story after story of people who have been fighting for justice, loving their neighbors, caring for widows and children, advocating for the vulnerable, spreading the gospel, and building the kingdom. This is where we want to make sure to say, Yay, church! 'Attaway to get after it and be the hands and feet of Jesus.

Even still, there are battles aplenty, and what's happening at the base of all those hills, so to speak, needs to get settled so that people can move in the direction of freedom and healing. But here's the rub: Instead of giddy-upping to the top of the hill and praying / advocating for repentance and change, many of us who could raise a staff on someone's behalf are strangely content to sit back while the carnage piles up. It's not that we aren't sympathetic. But it takes a lot of energy to get in the fray, and maybe we're so afraid of change, of losing our perceived ground, that the status quo feels comfortable.

I'm gonna counter that approach with two words.

But Jesus.

He is always the better Way. And do you know what we never, ever see Jesus do? Not ever—not even one time?

Ignore the hard thing because it might be inconvenient.

We've got to get in it, y'all.

I can only guess what your "it" is. But here's where I am.

For the last couple of years—ever since a white supremacy rally in Charlottesville, Virginia—I've been both mindful and convicted that I needed to do a lot less talking and a lot more listening. I specifically realized that I needed to be listening to more diverse voices—voices better acquainted with disenfranchisement and pain, voices engaged in church culture outside of my suburban bubble. And roughly twenty-four months later, here's my very succinct reaction to what I have read and heard and learned so far (not just about Charlottesville, not just about racism, but about any injustice, prejudice, abuse, or preoccupation with power that might threaten the integrity of the church, that might undermine the innate worth of image-bearers all around us):

> *Lord, forgive me. Forgive us.*
>
> *We've pretended for far too long that these battles were over and done.*
>
> *But the battles are still right in front of us—and we have mostly looked the other way.*

I grew up in central Mississippi, a part of the state that was a battleground for the Civil Rights Movement back in the 1960s. As a child, though, I didn't know much about the bombs and the brutality and the bloodshed that blighted the Magnolia State in the years before I was born. I knew about the Ku Klux Klan—I knew they were the bad guys—but I didn't have a lot of understanding about how people fought for voting rights, fought for equal rights, fought for integration, fought for black children to be afforded the same rights and privileges as white children. Not to be glib about it, but it just wasn't a topic that came up very often on the kindergarten playground.

Plus, when I started first grade, schools were integrated, and I didn't have any reason to think or know that it hadn't always been that way. I just knew that my friends were Vicki and Vel and Julie and Albert. It was nowhere on my radar that, even ten years prior, we wouldn't have been able to attend the same school.

I was probably in fourth or fifth grade when I started to hear firsthand accounts of the Civil Rights Movement, stories of heroism, stories of standing up for what was good and right and true right there in my own hometown. I also heard stories that frightened me, stories that made my stomach turn whenever we'd drive by a piece of property that was said to be owned by a KKK member. And when I was just a little bit older, I heard a story about something that happened in Philadelphia, Mississippi—maybe twenty-five miles down the road— that grieves me even now.

You've probably heard this story, too. In the Freedom Summer of 1964, Civil Rights workers were coming to Mississippi from all over the country to try to register black voters. Three men—James Chaney, a Mississippian, along with Andrew Goodman and Michael Schwerner, both from New York—were working with the voter registration drive, and one day they traveled to visit with a congregation from a church that had been burned near Philadelphia. Afterwards the three men were arrested in Philadelphia for speeding. When they were released from jail several hours later, they left town in their car, but they were pulled over, abducted, shot, and buried.

No one discovered their bodies for two months.

When I heard about these murders—a case that the FBI referred to as Mississippi Burning—I went straight to my mama. I wanted to know what she remembered, how she felt, what she did—anything that might give such an unthinkable event a more personal context. I'll never forget the beginning of our conversation.

"Mama," I asked, "do you remember when the Civil Rights workers were killed?"

"Yes," she answered. She closed her eyes and shook her head from side to side. We were standing in the kitchen.

"Mama? What did you do?"

"I hung my head in shame," she said. "I hung my head in shame."

Here's why I tell you that story.

All these years later, Mama's answer continues to echo in my ears and most especially in my heart. I'm convinced it's the way most of us respond when God opens our eyes to critical issues and injustices that demand the church's loving attention and care. For me, that issue was racism in general and systemic racism in particular. For you, it could be one of a million other things. But our response can sometimes be the same when God confronts us with something that breaks our heart. We hang our heads. We grieve. We feel ashamed for what we've done or left undone. We may even pretend the problem doesn't actually exist, because then we don't have to face it. And while I don't have any reason to think this was the case with Mama, I know what is most often true for myself: I feel ashamed for the ways I've been complicit, for the times I've looked the other way, for the platitudes I've offered instead of actual commitment and action.

I feel ashamed for when I've languished at the bottom of the hill, unsure about what to do while the battle rages all around. So I've looked down at the ground, and while I may have been sad—while I may have even been sympathetic—ultimately I haven't been very helpful.

For those of you who have found yourself in a similar spot, here's what I want to say to us.

People of God, lift up your head.

And if you feel like you can't, well—*people of God, ASK HIM TO LIFT IT.*

Because here's what I've been asking myself for the last couple of years: if I started to put the pretending of my younger years behind me that day on my kitchen floor, how do I intend to respond to this *collective* pretending? How do I offer help with the wounds and the battles and the injustices that many of us in the church have mostly continued to ignore? How should I participate in that?

And I will tell you where I've landed as a result of my listening.

I want to fight.

I don't want to just hang my head and be sad about it.

I want to fight.

To be clear, I don't want to just fight against a bunch of stuff. I don't want to be ruled by my anger. I want to fight *for* something, *for* someone, *for* the cause of the kingdom in the here and the now.

And as best I can, I want to continue to listen and learn what help is actually helpful.

So. We may not like facing it, but as the body of believers, we've done more than our fair share of pretending. We've pretended that our actions don't hurt others, that our policies don't hurt others, that our systems don't hurt others, that our leaders don't hurt others, that what we refuse to see doesn't hurt others.

And don't miss this: All that pretending has worked out pretty well for some folks in power because it's prevented the changes they fear.

But I'll tell you what I believe with my whole heart, not because I'm speaking from some high and mighty place, but because I know the cost of pretending: By refusing to acknowledge the battles that are right in front of us, brothers and sisters, we are wallowing in false peace. We're bathing in it. We're rubbing it behind our ears and between our toes and then telling ourselves it doesn't reek to high heaven.

We need not kid ourselves, though, because the places where the church is willing to pretend—the places where we equate the absence of rumbling with the presence of peace—it flies in the face of Shalom.

Lift up your head, people of God.

Whether we enter directly into the fray or climb the hills so we can come alongside our brothers and sisters, let's do it together. Fight. Raise the staff. Admit when we're weak. Ask for help.

And when someone *needs* our help, when we see brothers or sisters who are fighting the good fight and desperate for support as they grow battle-weary or work to make their way up hills too steep to walk alone, may we be quick to stand beside them—to stand all the way up for them—and lift their arms.

Remember, the Israelites weren't fighting for power.

They were fighting for dadgum deliverance.

May we be brave enough that the same will be said of us.

Lord, may the same be said of us.

Amen.

Perhaps I Should Put Down the Matches

I feel like I need to mention something that has been going on while I've been writing this book.

I'll try to keep it short-ish. You're so close to the end, after all.

My initial dream for book five (that's this one) was to call it *Burn It All Down*. I wanted to voice all the things that were making me angry and all the places I was beyond frustrated and all the ways, basically, that I was very right when other people were very wrong.

Cooler heads prevailed, of course. And the Lord has been kind to give me a couple of different pauses in the writing process so that I could consider whether the direction I was headed was beneficial to anyone, whether it was helpful to anything other than my seemingly endless need to vent and rant and complain.

Right or wrong, it's been a challenging time for my peacemaker personality.

Writing this book has been therapeutic—confirmation that the Lord hasn't left me during all the hard stuff. But about a week ago,

I started to hit an emotional wall. I've mentioned that I cry about three times a year, but last week I started crying because I had several emotional conversations in quick succession, and once the crying got going, I felt like I couldn't stop.

Yes. I realize that sounds oh-so-dramatic. It's certainly not how I like to operate, especially since I have a lot of pride and identity tied up in being a Certified Low-Maintenance Individual™. But it was like someone turned on a faucet that I couldn't turn off, and whenever the tears would slow to a trickle, I couldn't seem to get past one very repetitive thought.

I am so angry.

I am so angry.

I am so angry.

For as long as I can remember, anger has been a difficult emotion for me, mainly because I have no idea what to do with it. My initial reaction in a heated situation is to get as far away from the conflict as I can, and I've been that way since I was a little girl. Nobody wants to read my personal compendium of family arguments—and really, in the event of familial tension, we tended to favor icy silence over "a bunch of carryin' on," as my mama might have said—but the few times I remember active, bordering-on-loud disagreement, I felt like the world was falling apart. To this day I am deeply uncomfortable with people directing their anger at each other, so when I feel angry— whether it's justified or not—my go-to strategy is to avoid it, to push it down, to smile, and to *phrase my words very carefully.*

Here's the deal: I don't ever want to be ruled by my anger; I don't want it to make me impulsive or unloving or hard-hearted. So even though it might not make sense to people who engage with anger more easily, I am mostly able to talk myself out of it. I tell myself I shouldn't feel that way. I remind myself not to damage relationships in the heat of the moment. And to be completely honest, I likely engage with some internal narrative that my anger isn't ladylike or polite.

I sort of hate myself for that last one, by the way.

But it's a real thing.

So the fact that anger has piled up like it has over the last several years has been problematic, to say the least. It's been like a festival of repressed feelings, only the festival isn't fun at all and you might be sad to learn that there are no bands whatsoever.

Also they're completely out of water.

So it's pretty much just an empty field, some simmering rage, and a whole lot of heat.

David and I bought our current (and likely forever) house back in 2006. The house was built in 1974, so from the minute we signed closing papers, we've had a house-related to-do list. We've tackled more than our fair share of projects over the years—installing new kitchen countertops, replacing appliances, refacing kitchen cabinets, etc.—and this past summer, we decided it was time to tackle some painting we had put off for too long.

The house is forty-five years old at this point. Straight-up middle aged. Deferred maintenance can be a risky proposition.

So at the beginning of June, painters arrived, and *man oh man* did they ever transform the inside of our home. They painted several rooms, but the biggest change was in our living room. Our walls used to be a dark green-ish blue, a color I loved when we moved in and didn't necessarily think about changing. I lived with it for so long that I sort of forgot that I *could* change it.

My friend Grant helped me pick out new colors for the inside of the house, and as soon as our painter friends finished the first coat of Manchester Tan in the living room, I was blown away. Everything was lighter. Cleaner. Airier. The difference was dramatic in ways we never anticipated, and even now, the change in that room absolutely astounds me.

When the inside painting was finished, the painters began work on the outside. We painted everything a charcoal gray—wood, trim, eaves, posts, you name it—with the exception of our front door and sidelights, which we painted a beautiful dark orange.

Listen. The house may be forty-five years old, but as far as her paint is concerned, sis is KICKIN' IT right now.

May the same be said of my NARS-covered face.

Bless the Lord.

Not long after the exterior of our house was done, I started working on redecorating my office at school. Two of my (kind!) (generous!) coworkers had painted the walls earlier in the summer, so I set about the business of ordering new chairs, picking out fabric, selecting rugs, figuring out how to rearrange the furniture, and all of that fun stuff. My friend Heather helped me get everything ready before school started, and gosh it felt rewarding to have put all that effort into decorating and fluffing and brightening the places where I live and love and serve every day.

What a relief for everything to *look* better, you know?

I rested in the peace of everything looking better for five whole weeks, until one morning when David texted me a picture of our bathroom ceiling. There were two places with water damage, and when he called someone to come take a look, the repairman saw a large patch of water damage next to our shower. It must have happened recently since we had never noticed it, and on closer examination, the repairman realized that the water had been running into our basement, soaking the joists and the floor below. The leak seemed to be coming from inside our shower, and the repairman suggested that we contact a restoration specialist, someone who could fix the leak and repair the damage the best way.

A few days later, David and I met the kindest restoration specialist at our house so he could take a look at the issues in our bathroom. Within fifteen minutes he had looked at the ceiling and at the wall beside our shower. He went down to the basement to see what was going on with the joists, then looked inside the shower to assess what the problem might be.

The ceiling was going to be an easy fix, he said—just a regular ole leak from the roof. The problem with the shower leak, however, was more complicated. Even patching the leak would require the removal of a whole bunch of tile, not to mention replacing the soaked-through sheetrock and dealing with the problems in the basement. His suggestion—and David and I agreed—was to gut the shower and the wall beside it. Better to tear out the tile and liner and everything surrounding the leak, ensuring that any residual damage was addressed, than to essentially put a Band-Aid on the problems. A superficial fix might move faster and seem easier, but gutting and restoring was a wiser strategy for the long-term health and service of the shower.

The restoration specialist told us that he would send an estimate later that evening, and after he did just that, David and I talked it over. We both believed gutting the shower was the way to go, and the next morning, David emailed a signed agreement to begin the work.

Here's what the Lord has been reminding me ever since, especially in regard to my anger:

I want to be like the living room or the outside of the house or my office at school. I want to be able to make superficial changes—fluff up things a bit, maybe fake an extra measure of cheer—and not deal with whatever rot or damage lies beneath the surface. I want the quicker fix, the option where it doesn't take long for me to look shinier and smilier, where I don't have to give much thought to what is really lurking below all the shine and smiles.

Unfortunately, I'm much more like our shower. I tell myself that my anger isn't an issue, that it doesn't really matter. I tell myself that I'm justified in being frustrated with the church, in being disappointed with our nation's leadership, in being fed up with minority groups being systemically marginalized, and in being downright resentful about the ways women in and out of the church have been dismissed and discredited and dishonored. I really do believe that these things grieve the heart of God. But here's the reality: the anger has become so consistent and persistent that it's increasingly difficult for me to manage it in ways that are helpful and constructive. And what I know—just like I know how the water in our shower is damaging the wall that's supposed to support it—is that my anger seeps into the most significant parts of my life. It damages my mind and my soul and my relationship with the Lord.

I want so badly just to make everything look pretty, to pretend like that's enough.

But what I need is restoration.

My unexpected Cry-A-Thon led to deep conversations with some of the people who know me best: David, Heather, Kasey, Steph, and Shawn, my boss. I couldn't explain why the anger seemed like it had overwhelmed me, why on some level all of it felt mostly like grief. My people encouraged me to take some time to sort it out. Shawn wisely said, "You need to go through it, not around it," so I took him up on that. And last Thursday afternoon I drove home knowing two things for sure: I needed to spend time with the Lord, and I wanted to get face-to-face with my friends Angela and Travis, who live in Tennessee, along with my friend/mentor Anne, who lives here in Birmingham.

I couldn't have told you why any of this mattered. I didn't understand why five people I love and trust agreed that I needed to step back for a few days. I didn't know what I might find at the bottom of it all. But I knew this: sitting around with tears rolling down my face wasn't a sustainable option. Feeling perpetually angry wasn't a sustainable option. Being annoyed by things that normally brought me joy wasn't a sustainable option. So trusting the Lord's guidance through those friends seemed like the next right decision.

(And to be clear, I knew that I wasn't depressed. I knew I wasn't dealing with a situation that required medical attention. So if you *are* in a situation that requires medical attention—if you are so sad that getting out of bed is a struggle or you can't seem to move out of a dark place in your mind—please tell a friend and get to a doctor as soon as possible.)

(Also, you are deeply loved.)

(Just wanted to make sure to say that.)

The Lord gave me my first clue about what was up when I was reading my Bible the following Saturday morning. In Acts 20 Paul was saying goodbye to the elders at Ephesus, and toward the end of his remarks, he made a comment that leapt off the page at me: "But I consider my life of no value of myself; my purpose is to finish my course and the ministry I received from the Lord Jesus, to testify to the gospel of God's grace" (v. 24).

I'll tell you something. On the eve of fifty, thinking about how I hope to "finish my course" in life and in ministry, it resonates. And as soon as I read Paul's words, I felt a certainty in my spirit that this was part of the battle at hand. How do I want to run this leg of my race? Do I really want to testify to the gospel of God's grace? Or on some level am I more content to scream at the waves?

I didn't think I was a wave screamer, y'all. Color me surprised.

Sunday afternoon I hit the road for Angela and Travis's house, armed with a new worship playlist and a sermon Angela sent me before I left Birmingham. The four-hour drive passed pretty quickly—and that sermon hit me in the center of my heart—but I couldn't help but wonder if I was being silly, if I was overreacting, if there was any real point to driving such a long distance when I wouldn't even be there for twenty-four hours. This, by the way, is where I think the enemy gets all up in our heads when we're walking through something difficult; he convinces us that we don't need to tell anyone, we don't need to talk through it with anyone, and, in my case, that we're being unnecessarily high-maintenance to enlist the help of other people (much less to sacrifice our time) to try to get to the other side.

But I kept driving.

Sunday night Angela, Travis, and I sat around their kitchen table while I vented about everything that was on my dadgum nerves. I was still battling the feeling that it had been foolish to drive all that way, but since I hadn't been able to get the phrase "I am so angry" out of my head a couple of days before, I figured it might help to name specifically what was bothering me, to try to get to the heart of this dumb issue that was taking up so much dumb time and wasting so much of my dumb energy.

You know what seems easier than dealing with anger? *Pretending to be cheerful.*

Right before we went to bed that night, though, we were talking through some highs and lows of life, and Angela said something that caught my attention. It was almost an aside—something she said more to herself than to Travis and me—but she might as well have shouted:

"No matter where I am or what I'm doing, I just want to carry the presence of Jesus with me."

Well.

Then.

I mean.

Honestly.

I don't know how long it has been since that was the genuine posture of my heart—the sincere desire of my soul—but I can assure you that it has been a minute.

The next morning Angela and I sat down at her breakfast table, bleary-eyed from sleeping later than normal and, in my case, at least, delayed caffeine intake. While Angela cooked turkey sausage and eggs, I hovered over my coffee like it was the well of life and godliness, and after she sat down for breakfast, we picked up our conversation from the night before.

I can't remember our direct path, but there was a point when Angela mentioned the connection between faith and hearing, and she said, "Isn't something about that in Psalm 40? Can you read Psalm 40 out loud?"

So I did. And when I got to verse 11—"As for you, O LORD, you will not restrain your mercy from me; your steadfast love and your faithfulness will ever preserve me!" (ESV)—my voice caught in my throat. I was struck by a fresh awareness that as I was trying to figure out / pray through / work through the anger and frustration that had settled on me, the Lord was with me. The Lord would continue to be merciful. The Lord would see me through.

Angela and I talked and pondered and analyzed into the afternoon; her insight was calming, illuminating, and incredibly helpful. As I left Jackson I realized that it was day five of Sharing All the Feelings with Trusted Friends, and the vulnerability hangover was real. I continued to pray and process as I drove back to Birmingham, and not long before bed, I read a text from Heather that would get an A+ in the "edifying and encouraging" department. I wanted so badly to ingest her words like medicine, to let them settle over and into my heart, but it was almost like I was reading about a stranger. And when I wrote Heather back to thank her for her text and her friendship, I included my honest reaction to her kind words:

"I cannot see it, I cannot see it, I cannot see it."

That wasn't false humility. That was the straight-up truth.

The next morning I went back to Psalm 40, back to the words I had read aloud at Angela's kitchen table. When I got to verse 12, three words jumped out at me: "I cannot see" (ESV).

The same words I'd written to Heather the night before.

And when I looked at the beginning of the sentence to find the context of why David (the king, not my husband) couldn't see, I sat up in my chair. David said he couldn't see because "my iniquities have overtaken me," and when I read his words, I felt like a detective who had unearthed a major clue.

My iniquities have overtaken me.

My anger has blinded me to the goodness of God and His people.

I pulled out my journal and began to list all the ways my anger had been blinding me. To be clear, many of the things that poured out on the page were legitimate issues to be upset over. It's not wrong to care deeply about what's going on in the world because 1) some of it is heartbreaking 2) some of it is legitimately horrible. I'm good with not being okay with all of that stuff. However, when those issues create anger that is eating us up from the inside out, we are compromised. We can't be agents of change because we're too busy fuming and screaming and ranting and railing. Yes, there is a lot of sin "out there" that needs to be called out for what it is, but the Lord was gracious to remind me that there's also a lot of sin "in here" that needs to be called out and dealt with too. And when I actually listed out all the ways I've been blinded by anger, THERE WAS A LOT, my friends. I eventually got up from the table to take Hazel outside for a quick walk, and it was almost like I was thinking in bullet points, one epiphany after another. I continued to write it all down after we went back inside; for the first time in a while, clarity was rolling in like a river. Something significant had shifted, and I think it was this: I finally identified my anger as sin instead of a struggle.

Scripture had moved me from feeling to confessing.

There's such a big difference between the two, right? Feelings prompt me to turn to friends for comfort, but confession points me to the only One who can heal.

Changing my feelings makes for a nice little make-over.

Confessing my sin leads to full-blown restoration.

And when it comes to dealing with all my yuck and my bitterness and my anger, I don't just want to be helped; I want to be healed.

I want to see.

It's just like Angela had said the day before when we were sitting around her kitchen table: "If Jesus didn't come to change us, then what's the point?"

Tomorrow the restoration specialist is sending a crew to tear out our bathroom. Shower, sinks, vanity, mirrors, cabinets—it's all coming out. They're taking it down to the studs.

And what we didn't know a week ago is that there's all kinds of gunk behind the walls. There's moisture and mildew and apparently even a little bit of mold. It will take some careful cleaning and intensive care to fully restore what's damaged and broken.

But our restoration specialist, he has it covered.

So does our Restoration Specialist. Granted, He isn't sending out a crew (I'm smiling), but He's definitely at work—through Scripture, through the Holy Spirit, through His people. He truly wants to move all of us who trust in Him in the direction of confession and repentance and restoration; He is very deliberately demolishing the stuff that has no place in His kingdom. By His grace, He is changing us. And by His grace, when we're compelled to fight for justice or build relational bridges or speak up for people who can't, we can stand up as believers who are filled with His peace and His presence.

Instead of, you know, white-hot rage.

Here's our part of this deal, though: we have to make room. We have to confess the junk that would hold us in our pride and our anger and our fear and our bitterness. We have to let Him have His way with it. Otherwise we're just one more clanging cymbal in a world that is already overwhelmed with noise.

But in the midst of all the noise, the Spirit is moving. The Spirit is loving. The Spirit is clear.

And as I've processed and prayed through and confessed my anger, I've realized something: I really don't want to burn it all down.

I want holy fire to fall.

So here's to the confessing and the repenting and the renouncing and the agreeing and the restoring that will change us from the inside out. That will rip out our anger and entitlement and rightness from the roots. That will strip us of our arrogance and heal our blindness and send us into the world standing tall as agents of love and mercy and justice.

That will make us more like Jesus.

His kingdom come.

His will be done.

On earth, as it is in heaven.

Notes

1.   https://www.rollingstone.com/music/music-features/eric-church -desperate-man-nashville-country-700750/.

2. brookhills.org—sermon from 2/3/19.

3. *Matthew Henry Commentary*, https://www.biblegateway.com/passage /?search=Exodus+17&version=ESV.

Acknowledgments

This book took a little longer than normal to write, and that is because I lost the first 20,000 words after I spilled a very tall glass of Crystal Light on my computer and drowned my memory sticks (cards? buckets?) in a pool of artificially sweetened lemon water. I didn't have any back-ups of my work because I never envisioned a scenario where I would lose the first 20,000 words of my book and also I WAS VERY FOOLISH (however, the School of Hard Knocks featuring Crystal Light has taught me some lessons). Anyway, my point is that this book required a little extra encouragement and TLC, mostly because losing twenty thousand words will make you want to get up in the bed with a bag of Cheetos and seven to twenty-three seasons of assorted reality television programming downloaded on your iPad. The fact that I started over (and finished!) testifies to the support and kindness and general YOU CAN DO ITs of some people who mean the world to me.

So. My heartfelt thanks and deepest appreciation to the amazing group of women who have loved, cheered, and led in ways that flat-out made it possible for me to keep on writing: Jean Castille,

Nicole Conrad, Stephanie Coons, Angela Cottrell, Sara Foust, Jamie Golden, Ashley Gorman, Jen Hatmaker, Suzanne Heidepriem, Lisa Jackson, Heather Mays, Delinda Merry, Kasey Mixon, Erin Moon, Beth Moore (along with her straight fire Twitter feed), Anne Reddick, Melanie Shankle, and Amanda Tindall. Not to mention my beloved college friends (current events therapy with Daph has been critical), social media friends, *Big Boo Cast* listeners, and Hazel Hudson (just FYI—Hazel is our dog, but she is always v. v. affectionate when I am v. v. discouraged, and that is some timely snuggling).

Thanks to Shawn Brower, David Conrad, Joey Coons, Landon Gray, Guy Hensley, Joel Mixon, and Bryan White. I am deeply grateful for your friendship.

Thanks to Daddy, Sister, and Brother for being so willing to share Mama's story—and for trusting me with so many of our family's stories. As we all know, the Sims / Davis combo is a little bit of a narrative goldmine. :-)

Also, I am forever indebted to Alex Hudson, who delights me at every turn and never let my little Crystal Light snafu interfere with his desire to make some jokes—and David Hudson, who encourages my writing more than anyone and never once shamed me about not backing up my files even though I feel certain he still has a floppy disk with our Quicken checkbook transactions from 1998 in a box somewhere in our garage. I love you both. You're my favorite people.

To the those of you who just finished reading this book (whether that is by choice or under some significant pressure from your book club), I cannot thank you enough. Your time is precious, and I'm so honored to have spent a few hours with you. It is not lost on me that you could have been watching one of the 478 streaming services instead. It's a privilege to have been welcomed into your dens and lunch breaks and carpool lines and beach chairs. I am humbled and grateful for the invitation.

Finally, I started writing this book (both times!) with such a heavy heart. Life has been confusing and wonderful and painful and glorious and heartbreaking and occasionally even embarrassing these last few years. I can honestly say that Jesus has loved me and taught me through every bit of it. He is faithful, kind, merciful, and loving. As the world shakes, He holds. He's the reason I stand.

> *But I do not account my life of any value nor as precious to myself, if only I may finish my course and the ministry that I received from the Lord Jesus, to testify to the gospel of the grace of God.* (Acts 20:24 ESV)

About the Author

Sophie Hudson loves stories. She also loves to laugh, which means that writing funny stories and getting to share them with other people is basically a dream come true. Sophie hopes that her stories help women find encouragement and hope in the everyday, joy-filled moments of life, and she also hopes that her readers will laugh until it hurts just a little bit. When she's not writing or cohosting The Big Boo Cast, Sophie is likely searching for the perfect pair of pajama pants, attending a live sporting event, or binge-watching a TV show in record time. She lives with her husband and son in Birmingham, Alabama.

You can follow her on the interwebby social sites.

Twitter	@boomama
Instagram	@boomama205
Facebook	@SophieHudsonBooMama
Blog	BooMama.net
Favorite podcast app	The Big Boo Cast